Death and Grief
A Guide for Clergy

Alan Wolfelt, Ph.D.
Director
Center for Loss and Life Transition
Fort Collins, Colorado

ACCELERATED DEVELOPMENT
A member of the Taylor & Francis Group

DEATH AND GRIEF
A GUIDE FOR CLERGY

Library of Congress Catalogue Card Number: 88-070009

International Standard Book Number: 0-915-202-76-X

Printed in United States of America

Technical Development: Tanya Dalton
Delores Kellogg
Marguerite Mader
Sheila Sheward

For additional information and ordering, please contact:

ACCELERATED DEVELOPMENT
A member of the Taylor & Francis Group
1900 Frost Road, Suite 101, Bristol, PA 19007
1-800-821-8312

DEDICATION

To Sue, who helps me live life
with meaning and purpose

In memory of Tia Burridge
May 30, 1975—July 14, 1985

92829

PREFACE

Death is not an enemy to be conquered or a prison to be escaped. It is an integral part of our lives that gives meaning to human existence. It sets a limit on our time in this life, urging us to do something productive with that time as long as it is ours to use. When you fully understand that each day you awaken could be the last you have, you take time that day to grow, to become more of who you really are, to reach out to other human beings.

E. Kübler-Ross, J. Braga, L. Braga[1]

My hope is that this book will serve as a source of encouragement and practical help to those clergy who want an understandable framework in which to view their helping role with grieving persons. Experience suggests that few helping situations are more challenging, nor more rewarding, than the opportunity to assist persons impacted by loss in their lives.

The book has evolved out of my work as an educator and clinician in the area of thanatology. During the last decade I have had the privilege of being asked to teach clergy and other caregivers what grieving adults, children, and families have taught me about compassionate helping. Recently, clergy of a variety of faiths who have participated in my workshop and lecture presentations, have encouraged me to write down the many questions and responses that have grown out of our discussions. I thank these clergy-persons for their supportive encouragement.

Death and Grief: A Guide for Clergy has been written to assist in filling what I perceive as a need for a compact yet comprehensive text for clergy who wish to enhance their ability to assist others during times of death and grief. Clergy are in a natural position to help people who experience a variety of developmental transitions. Historically, clergy have been involved as supporters of the bereaved since the beginning of time. And yet, many clergy tell me that their education lacked substantive teachings in the area of caring for the bereaved. Therefore, in attempting to respond to an apparent need, I am directing this text specifically toward clergy, while at the same time hoping that anyone involved in this area of caregiving will find the contents of value.

This book is not intended to make clergy* experts in the area of grief counseling. Such specializations would be the opposite of this author's belief that part of of a clergyperson's unique value lies in the capacity to be a generalist. A major purpose of this book is, instead, to create a climate of putting care in action within the church and community setting.

Clergy are among the few outreach oriented caregivers available to assist people in need. Hopefully, this text will help you feel more comfortable in your role of supportive counselor, educator, friend, and when appropriate, referral source to other care providers. Howard Clinebell, Jr., nicely stated his observations about the role of clergy as helper when he wrote: "There is no doubt that ministers occupy a central and strategic role as counselors in our society. It is obvious that clergymen [I hope he also meant clergywomen] are on the front lines in the struggle to lift the loads of troubled persons."[2]

While we do not yet, and I'm certain never will, totally possess all of the knowledge there is to know about grief, we do have a good start. Clearly, no one book, not this book, not any one book, will inform us about "everything there is to know about death and grief." Our own personal perspectives on death and grief will probably change and grow with each new loss we encounter. Loss, transition, and grief change us and create opportunities to learn about life and living, as well as, death and dying. Perhaps through deepening our human capacity to respond to each other in times of grief, we can continue to enrich each moment of our living.

The words written here are an effort to describe a continually evolving body of knowledge related to grief and to aid in the clergyperson's degree of helpfulness at this time. I have attempted to bring to this book practical information and principles gleaned from my personal experiences with loss, the body of literature available and my clinical practice with grieving persons. I would be remiss if I did not thank all of those bereaved persons who have shared their innermost thoughts and feelings with me over the past ten years. They have greatly enriched my teaching and my own

---

*The term "clergy" is used throughout text to describe all religious caregivers, including priests, rabbis and ministers.

personal experiences with loss. I also would like to credit and thank my colleagues within the field of thanatology for their desire to share the insights we now have about grief with as many caregivers as possible. Their writings, comments, and support have assisted me in deciding what to include in the content of this book.

For the purpose of ease of reading and quick reference to specific topic areas, a question and response format has been used for this text. My belief is that this will allow the reader to move to specific areas of interest and concern. As I began to write this book, a desire to provide a unique format in this form of a reference and training guide evolved. The question-response format seemed to best allow for the achievement of this goal.

However, this book does not promise a simple package of answers that can be provided for any death-grief situation encountered. It does offer information and principles of caregiving that when applied with knowledge, sensitivity, and caring should help make your life work even more rewarding.

Please note that this text does not include in-depth discussion of the general topics of dying or religion. The focus of the content is primarily on the psychological and social aspects of grief. This is not meant to infer that the religious background of a person is not an important determinate in the experience of one's grief. If the helper fails to acknowledge the influence of religious beliefs related to the expression of grief, there is an excellent chance of totally misunderstanding the persons who entrust you to assist them. My hope is that each of you, as clergy, bring your own personal faith, hope, and love to your helping role.

While without doubt, a number of reasons exist why people often turn to clergy for help with their grief. My own belief is that persons desire to be regarded in that special dimension of their humanity. In my thinking, the unique integrity of the pastoral relationship can provide for the acknowledgement of this humanity.

And so, we begin our journey toward enhancing our under-standing of what we have come to term grief. Perhaps before we begin we should remind ourselves that experience suggests the following: The capacity to provide grieving people with a sense of feeling understood is at the heart of all effective counsel. Understanding, communicated through the discipline of counseling skills, helps the grieving person see self in better perspective. My hope is that this book will help you as a clergyperson use the capacity of your own understanding in a measured, yet powerfully effective way. Shall we begin?

Alan D. Wolfelt, Ph.D.

Alan D. Wolfelt, Ph.D.
Center For Loss and Life Transition
Fort Collins, Colorado

REFERENCES

[1]   Kubler-Ross, E., Braga, J., & Braga, L. (1975). "Omega", *Death: The Final Stage of Growth.* Englewood Cliffs, NJ: Prentice Hall.

[2]   Clinebell, Jr., H.J. (1966). *Basic Types of Pastoral Counseling.* Nashville: Abingdon Press.

TABLE OF CONTENTS

LIST OF FIGURES

1

SEMANTIC DISTINCTIONS IN TERMINOLOGY

Could you define the terms bereavement, grief, and mourning?

An excellent starting point in attempting to provide a framework for the increased understanding of one's helping role is to simply make some semantic distinctions in these commonly used terms. However, we should acknowledge that words are inadequate in conveying the magnitude of these experiences.

Bereavement is a state caused by loss such as death. Numerous types of losses can bring about a state of bereavement.

Grief is an emotional suffering caused by death or another form of bereavement. Grief involves a sequence of thoughts and feelings that follow the loss and accompany mourning. Grief is a process and as a result, is not a specific emotion like fear or sadness, but indeed is a constellation of a variety of thoughts, feelings, and behaviors. Grief is the internal meaning given to the external event.

Mourning is the outward expression of grief and bereavement. The specific ways in which people mourn are influenced by the customs of their culture. The mourning behavior exhibited may or may not be in agreement with true feelings of the bereaved; however, they may incur disapproval if they do not follow the prescribed social customs. Another way of defining mourning is to state that it is "grief gone public" or "sharing one's grief outside of oneself."

Other related terms of which the caregiver should be aware are as follows:

Anticipatory Grief is most often used to describe grief that is expressed in advance of a loss when the loss is perceived as inevitable (see pages 131-133).

Acute Grief is the intense grief which immediately follows the loss.

Grief Work is the activity(s) associated with thinking through the loss, facing its reality, expressing the feelings and emotions experienced, and becoming reinvolved with life. The work of grief coincides with what has been termed the tasks of mourning.

Other significant terminology that aids in understanding essential concepts will be noted in the pages ahead.

Now that the preceding terms have been defined in a more formal sense, lets take a moment to acknowledge that grief is a much more personal experience than their words describe. For example, grief is—waking up in the middle of the night and reaching out to touch someone who is no longer there. Grief is—hearing that special song, seeing that special place, and longing for that special person. And yes, grief is a mixture of adjustments, fears and uncertainties that confront life in its forward progress and make it difficult to reconcile and redirect the energies of life, of living, and of loving.

So grief is much more than words alone. Grief is real and it does not simply go away. Experiencing these complex emotions of grief is often movement through an unknown territory that is embraced by an overwhelming sense of pain and loss. And yet, in helping people move toward their grief, and experience it, one has the opportunity to be a catlyst for healing.

2

SOCIAL INFLUENCES
AND GRIEF

What is your perception of the social influences that relate to the expression of grief in our culture?

For many years the belief has been that human behavior is always a function of two sets of conditions, those involving the person and those involving the situation in which the person is living. As we observe grief in a social context today, it seems that our society frequently gives the message to grieving persons that their loss is not a matter of general concern. The grieving person is supposed to be *"strong"* and *"brave"* even when it is unhealthy to repress normal suffering and pain. The unfortunate consequence is that the grieving person is often left to his or her own resources at the very time those resources are the most depleted.

In our efforts to understand the individuals experience with grief, we must acknowledge that the social environment can either help or hinder the process. In this writer's clinical experience, negative social influences can, and frequently do, lead to a complicated journey through ones's grief.

Perhaps you have heard grief described as the emotions that heal themselves. While this may have been true at some point in history, we now realize that the majority of people need some supportive social context for healing to occur. Grievers need the opportunity to share their grief outside of themselves in a caring environment.

The unfortunate reality is that many grievers do not give themselves permission, or receive permission from others, to grieve, to express their many conflicting thoughts and feelings. We live in a society that often encourages the repression of the emotions of grief, as opposed to the expression. The result is that many people either grieve in isolation, or attempt to run away from their grief through various means.

During ancient times, stoic philosophers encouraged their followers not to mourn, believing that self control was the appropriate response to sorrow. Still today, well intentioned, but uninformed people carry on this long held tradition. A vital task of the helper is to encourage and support the outward expression of grief. The grieving person moves toward reconciling self to the loss when he or she can attend to his or her emotional experiences, accepting them as a result of the privilege of having been capable of loving another person. A renewed sense of well being has the opportunity to evolve as caring people accept the grievers for who they are, as they are, where they are. Grief is a time for the expression of normal emotions.

Does this lack of a supportive social context you have described influence people's perception of how long grief should last?

Absolutely and without a doubt. One of the reasons for many people's preoccupation with the very question; "How long does grief last?" often relates to society's impatience with grief. Shortly after the funeral the grieving person is expected to "be back to normal." Persons who continue to express grief outwardly are often viewed as "weak," "crazy," or "self-pitying." The common message is "shape up and get on with your life." Grief is something to be overcome rather than experienced.

The result of these kinds of messages is to encourage the repression of the griever's thoughts and feelings. Refusing to allow tears, suffering in silence, and "being strong," are thought to be admirable behaviors. An unresponsive society can result in a heightened sense of isolation and aloneness in the grieving person.

Many grieving people have internalized society's message that grief should be done quietly and quickly. Returning to the routine of work shortly after the death of someone loved, the widow relates, "I'm fine," in essence saying "I'm not mourning." Friends, family, and co-workers relieved by her stance admire her apparent strength and refrain from talking with her about her loss. The bereaved person having an apparent absence of mourning tends to be more socially accepted by those around him or her.

However, this type of collaborative pretense surrounding grief does not meet the emotional needs of the bereaved person. Instead, she is likely to be further isolated with her grief, with the eventual onset of the "going crazy syndrome." Attempting to mask and repress her feelings of grief, results in internal anxiety and confusion. The world outside of the person continues to go on in its usual way. With little, if any, tolerance for her own grief, combined with lack of social recognition and support, the woman begins to think her thoughts and feelings are abnormal and that she is in fact, "going crazy." As a matter of fact, the most frequent initial presentation of grieving persons at our Center for Loss and Life Transition in Colorado is the statement, "I think I'm going crazy."

The lack of expression of outward mourning has brought about the evolution of the "silent mourner." Often, even those persons who want to be supportive cannot identify the mourner. The relegating of grief to behind closed doors reinforces the importance of being outreach oriented with ones helping efforts.

In summary, our society frequently fails to support the bereaved person, particularly during the lengthy transition period after the funeral. An emphasis on being rational and staying under control influences mourners to reintegrate into the social network and keep their tears, fears, and hurts to themselves. We must work to reverse this trend that fails to acknowledge the continuing need for support and understanding of the bereaved. My hope is that this text is a step toward allowing readers to better achieve this goal.

NOTES

3

INCREASED INTEREST IN BEREAVEMENT CARE

Clergy, as well as other caregivers, appear to have an increased interest in the area of bereavement care— why do you think this has occurred?

The recent increased interest in the area of bereavement care has been accompanied by a general increase in interest in a wide range of issues related to death and dying. In the past twenty-five years, the importance of learning from the experiences of loss in our lives has evolved in both the social sciences (psychology, sociology, and anthropology), and the biological sciences (medicine and biology). Thanatology, the study of death, dying and grief has become an interdisciplinary field. Each discipline brings a perspective that makes for a greater whole.

Religious institutions and the clergy have been involved with the bereaved throughout history. Interesting to note is that this relatively new found interest in death, dying, and grief for clergy and other caregivers, is really a resurgence of interest that has been present since the beginning of time. The book titled, *The Art of Dying* was first written in the time of ancient Rome.

This realization that not everything related to the care of the dying and the grieving is new, actually helps give us perspective on what we are doing today. For example, we can very easily observe that with the more recent popularization of the study of death or the onset of what Robert Kastenbaum has termed the "Death Awareness Movement" we have witnessed an almost superficial or fad-like interest in the topics of death, dying, and grief. Unfortunately, the very persons who often treat death with this fad-like interest are the ones who begin to prescribe to others how to die and how to grieve. In addition, a frequent discovery related to persons who evoke a superficial understanding of grief is that they have not encountered any personal experience with loss.

As to why the new found interest, we can look to a combination of factors. Many people, both lay and professional, have demonstrated an urge to learn more about something that has been avoided in years past. Our dissension of death in the not so distant past has been marred by euphemistic language, by isolation of the dying, and repression of the right and value of grieving. Currently, there is an awareness that a continued attitude of the denial of death will only serve to distance us more from life. An excellent rationale for more open, honest, approach to experiences of death and grief was provided by Octavio Paz, who wrote: "A civilization that denies death ends by denying life."[1]

Historical events of this century also have helped force us to confront our own mortality—two world wars, the atomic bomb, a prolonged war in Vietnam, assassination of political leaders, international terrorism, and the potential of nuclear holocaust. These events have made maintaining a facade of indifference to the realities of death and grief more difficult. The threat of nuclear war alone should provide a catalyst for discussion of a wide range of topics related to thanatology.

Clearly, our present upsurge in interest in death, dying, and grief is one of transition. Death, dying, and bereavement have become more acceptable topics for public discussion. Published in 1959, Herman Feifel's book, *The Meaning of Death*[2], brought together a number of authors from a variety of disciplines whose writings encompassed theoretical approaches, cultural and religious concepts, developmental and attitudinal studies, and clinical aspects of death. Beginning with Fiefel's text, death began to be accepted as an area of investigation to be explored by scholars, clinical practitioners, and the lay public.

In 1969, Elizabeth Kübler-Ross authored, *On Death and Dying*[3], which further stimulated the lay public's interest in learning more about death and dying. This text introduced the concept of stages in the dying process and has sold well over a million copies.

The lay public's willingness, if not eagerness to discuss death, became evident in a 1970 *Psychology Today* survey on the topic that resulted in over thirty thousand responses. This was more responses than the magazine had ever received to any prior surveys.

The 1970s and 80s have seen hundreds of articles and texts published on the general topics of dying, death, and grief, as well as more specialized topics such as children and death, suicide, the hospice movement, and the funeral industry. In response to the increased interest in thanatology, courses devoted specifically to the topic have been popular. Among other reasons, the events outlined above have contributed to an increased interest among a variety of professional persons, in addition to the lay public.

REFERENCES

[1] Paz, O. (1961). *The labyrinth of solitude: Life and thought in Mexico.* New York: Grove Press.

[2] Feifel, H. (1959). *The meaning of death.* New York: McGraw-Hill.

[3] Kübler-Ross, E. (1969). *On death and dying.* New York: Macmillan.

NOTES

4

BROADER FRAMEWORK FOR LOSS

I'm aware that we experience variety of loses in our lives. Could you provide a broader framework for acknowledging the different kinds of losses we encounter?

The experience of mourning losses in our lives is much more common than we often stop to realize. When we hear the word grief, we tend to most readily associate this word with death; however, we should note the different types of loss that are a basic part of living. We also may want to keep in mind that prior experience with loss of any type, influences how we experience the death of those that we love, as well as, impacts on the sense of loss we attach to our own death.

David Peretz[1] suggested that loss be grouped into four major catagories: the loss of a person, the loss of some aspect of self, the loss of external objects, and developmental losses.

THE LOSS OF A PERSON

The death of someone loved is often the most intense form of relationship loss. However, a variety of other relationship losses are also experienced as a part of life. Separation, divorce, and moves are but a few examples of relationship losses. In addition, aging and illness may result in the loss of a relationship with a person in the form we once knew it. Alzheimer's disease is an example of how we may experience the loss of the person as we once knew them.

Mitchell and Anderson[2] aptly described the loss of relationship when they wrote the following: "Relationship loss is the ending of opportunities to relate oneself to, talk with, share experiences with, make love to, touch, settle issues with, fight with, and otherwise be in the emotional and/or physical presence of a particular other human being."

THE LOSS OF SOME ASPECT OF SELF

This is wherein what we experience as loss exists within the self. "Self" meaning a general sense of identity or well-being. Many external losses that occur outside of us, like death, are accompanied by a "loss of self." The natural tendency is to define oneself by the relationships, roles, and ideas to which one is attached.

Examples of loss of some aspect of self includes the following: (1) loss of ideas, hopes, dreams; (2) loss of health and/or body function; (3) loss of self-esteem and positive self-attitude; (4) loss of belief system or faith; (5) loss of role, such as no longer being a spouse following death or no longer being an employee following retirement.

The reality that much overlapping and compounding of losses are easy to observe as we consider these losses related to self. One illustration is when upon the death of a significant loved person the survivor questions previously held belief systems, loss or role as spouse, and struggles with self-esteem issues. This combination of types of losses with which the mourner struggles is actually very common.

THE LOSS OF EXTERNAL OBJECTS

The majority of people naturally have meaningful attachments to some external objects(s) such as their home, land, or special treasured possessions. While we can often replace material possessions, that fact alone, does not negate the experience with loss and grief. Regardless of the capacity to replace the original lost object, for the majority of people, the replacement is never quite the same as the original. Anyone who has experienced the loss of valued objects to fire, flood, or other catastrophes can certainly attest to the significance of this type of loss.

DEVELOPMENTAL LOSSES

Loss is present from the moment of birth until the moment of death. In a very real sense, life becomes a series of losses. Developmental losses are those types of losses which occur in the process of normal human development. To name a few, the infant experiences the loss of the bottle or breast, the adolescent experiences the loss of early childhood, the parent experiences the loss of the last child moving away from home, the retired person experiences the loss of role function at work, and the aged adult experiences the decline in health often accompanied by loss of control over his/her environment. So, as previously written, life is a series of developmental losses. Therefore, if a person is going to live well, it would naturally make sense that he or she would need to mourn well. These expected, developmental losses are often traumatic for the person who has limited emotional and physical resources to reconcile these losses. We would never want to assume that just because a loss is expected that it is easy to work through.

The caregiver who is sensitive to the four broad catagories of loss outlines above, will be more prepared to offer helpful guidance and support.

REFERENCES

[1] Peretz, D. (1970). Development, Object-Relationships, and Loss. In Schoenberg, B., et al., *Loss and Grief*. New York: Columbia University Press.

[2] Mitchell, K.R., & Anderson, H. (1983). *All our losses: All our griefs*. Philadelphia: The Westmenster Press.

NOTES

5

ATTACHMENT INFLUENCES ON GRIEF

I realize that the experiences of grief is a function of attachment. Could you describe how attachment influences our experience with grief?

The work of John Bowlby, on attachment theory, illustrates that the experience of grief is not just a function of loss, but a function of the attachment of the survivor to the person who died. Grief is most often experienced in relation to the significance of the attachment. This helps explain why we see people who have had difficult relationships that end in death or divorce grieve just as acutely as those who have had happier relationships. Actually, relationships that end wherein strong components of ambivilence have been present are often among the most complicated of grief responses to reconcile.

Bowlby's theory of attachment has suggested the presence of certain human "species-specific" instincts or behaviors. Among his list of human instincts is smiling, crying, sucking, and attachment. Historically, Bowlby has been one of the leaders in the evolution of the ethological model for understanding grief. Bowlby, Charles Darwin, and Konrad Lorenz have studied these species-specific behaviors and asked: "What is the function of such behavior in the evolutionary development of that species?"

Studies on attachment, separation, and loss have indicated that attachment behavior is a life-long process that begins in childhood. Adult attachments are viewed as an extension of childhood affectional bonds. In that human beings need to form and maintain attachments continues throughout life, so too does our vulnerability to loss. Bowlby has noted, "This picture of attachment behavior as a normal and healthy component of man's instinctive equipment leads us also to regard separation anxiety as the natural and inevitable response when ever an attachment figure is unaccountably missing."[1]

In studying the disruption of bonding in young children, Bowlby observed what he described as a predictable sequence of grief-related behaviors. Specifically, he outlined a model that followed a three-phase pattern of (1) protest, (2) despair, and (3) detachment.

An illustration of Bowlby's pattern of grief is observed when the young child is separated from a parent for a prolonged period of time. Initially tears of *protest* may be present in hopes that the anguish expressed will lead to reunion with the caretaker. When the reality sets in that immediate reunion will not take place, the child withdraws into a sense of *despair.* Over time, if the separation is prolonged, the child forgets about the parent, resulting in *detachment,* even if and when the parent returns. Many of you have probably observed components of protest, despair, and detachment in your work with grieving persons.

In summary, if grief is a function of attachment, then as we begin to invest ourselves in another person, we allow ourselves to become vulnerable to loss. The more we allow ourselves to attach, the more potential we have of experiencing the painful emotions of grief. Simply stated, if we choose to love, we choose to grieve. You have probably observed some people who appear to decide not to love, either consciously or unconsciously, out of a fear of the loss they will encounter and the grief they will experience.

Sullender[2] has written of the clergy's role in relationship to encouraging parishioners to make attachments and how this inherently relates to the experience of grief.

> Religion has traditionally encouraged people to care, to get involved and "to love your neighbor." By so doing pastors are implicitly asking people to grieve as well. We should be clear about that. Grief is an inevitable part of love. The more we ask parishioners "to care", the more we are asking them to be willing to grieve. One cannot truly care without being hurt..... If we wish people to be "lovers" and caregivers, then we, as pastors, must help them learn how to grieve. Grief is a part of love. If our style of pastoral ministry tends to deny, avoid or repress grief feelings, then we will inevitably repress love as well. We will teach our congregation how to love, when we can teach them how to grieve.(pp 35,36)

As we have outlined attachment thinking in relationship to grief, then to me we need not teach ourselves and others how to avoid relationships, but instead, how to boldly enter into relationships. From our shared love comes meaning and from our experiences with grief and loss can come growth. If we do the work necessary to reconcile our losses, our ability to be enriched by new loves will invariably be enhanced.

Isn't there also a theory of object-relations that relates to the way we become attached to or detached from persons, places, or even ideas?

Yes, there certainly is. A general understanding of this particular theory assists in the task of helping the mourner. Let's provide ourselves with this general understanding of object relations thinking.

Object relations refers to those relations between an individual and the "things" in his or her environment wherein emotional significance is invested. In object relations thinking, the infant begins to distinguish between "self" and "primary objects," mother, father, siblings, peers, and external objects. The infant begins to develop the capacity to internalize a mental image of the person or object to which he/she has become attached. Therefore, even in the absence of the other person, the infant is able to maintain this internalized image.

For this "internalized construct" or mental image to occur in the child, a relatively consistent presence of this other person must be within the child's environment so that attachment can occur. Melanie Klien[3], one of the proponents of object relations thinking, has proposed that the development of a lively sense of self depends on having an internal world of reliable images to which one is attached.

When object attachment begins to occur and feelings are invested this internalized image is taken in and becomes a part of oneself. For example, in Figure 1 is symbolically outlined this process.

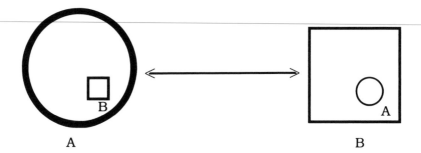

Figure 1. Internalized construct attachment.

In Figure 1 is depicted how person A, as well as person B, each has an internalized image of the other within oneself. Thus, when one of the two persons dies, the survivor is left with a part of the self that is experienced as lost. This actually helps explain the frequent comment of the newly bereaved: "When he died, I felt as if part of me died with him." In a very real sense, according to object relations theory and a phenomenological perspective, this remark is very true. Among the tasks of the mourner is to not only grieve the physical loss of the person, but also the internalized image of the other within oneself.

As previously outlined, if a person experiences the death of another whereby little emotional attachment has occurred, the task of mourning the real physical loss and the internalized image will not be great. However, if a meaningful emotional attachment has formed, the survivor must involve self in the work of mourning.

Can you depict through object relations, some of the ways in which the survivor mourns the lost person?

Yes, we can use some additional figures and descriptions of what they depict to aid in our understanding of what may occur. We will outline three areas that are frequently observed when we think about the survivor's task of detaching from the internalized construct or mental image of the lost person within oneself: (1) construct retention, (2) construct replacement, and (3) construct reconciliation.

Figure 2. Construct Retention.

In Figure 2 is depicted a normal process of the survivor temporarily retaining the internalized construct (image) of the person who has died. This is symbolically indicated by how the internalized image is the same size within the survivor as it was prior to the death of the other person. The length of time that the survivor psychologically needs to be able to retain this internalized image will vary depending upon a number of factors. For example, when the nature of the death is sudden and unexpected, the survivor will typically demonstrate the need to retain the image for a longer period of time as compared to the survivor who has anticipated the death of the significant other.

Construct retention relates to what is commonly termed shock, denial, numbness, and disbelief. For a period of time the mourner needs time to push away the reality that the person is no longer alive. Part of how the mourner achieves this "blocking out" is to retain the internalized image. Just as the process of attachment occurred over time, so too does the process of detachment. To attempt to prescribe the specific length of time the mourner should be allowed, if not encouraged to retain this internalized construct, is potentially damaging. Much more appropriate to the helping task would be to work to understand the person's underlying needs to retain the internalized image over time.

We also should note, that not all mourners should be expected to move away from construct retention and toward construct reconciliation. More specifically, the needs of the mourner to move toward reconciliation will vary due to unique circumstances, such as age. For example, the 75-year old person who has been married to their spouse for over fifty years may on occasion demonstrate an apparent lack of outward mourning as they work to keep their dead spouse alive through construct retention. Focusing on the memory of the spouse and allowing for retention may well best meet the needs of this bereaved older adult. In other words, we never want to assume that our task as helpers is to break through a person's defensive need to retain the internalized construct. Obviously, our therapeutic tasks with a 40-year old widow or widower, are different than they are with the 75-year old widow or widower.

A brief real life example seems appropriate here. Within the past year I was consulted by a nursing home regarding what the staff within the care facility was terming a pathological grief reaction in a 94-year old woman. At the time of my consultation, the woman had been bereaved for approximately six months, following the death of her husband. She and her husband had been married for 61 years and resided together in the nursing home during the past five years.

After asking the staff to inform me of their concerns about this woman, I, in the form of a summary, was told the following: "Since her husband's death, she really has not cried very much, but persistently talks about him as if he was still alive. She acknowledges that he is dead one day and then the next seems to talk as if she still feels very close to him. When she was allowed to go to the dining area to take meals, she almost invariably felt a need to talk about her dead husband with the residents and staff. Because of this, we have felt it best to not allow her out of her room during the past two months. After all, it's depressing to hear her talk about him, in part because we miss him too. Can you make her quit talking about her husband?"

Obviously, the staff became an additional focus of my consultation. Among the issues involved in this situation was the staff's need to protect themselves from their own emotions of grief, "it's depressing to hear her talk about him, in part because we miss him, too." So, out of the need to protect themselves from their own emotions, they created a repressed, closed environment whereby this woman was discouraged from talking about her husband. This is an example of how this woman needed to be allowed to maintain the construct retention of her husband. So what if at times she talked about him as if he was still alive. Certainly her memories of him were alive and as I got to know and learn from her, she taught me that being able to have these memories were in fact, what kept her alive. At times the older person's ability to make effective use of memories, is what invites them to go on living.

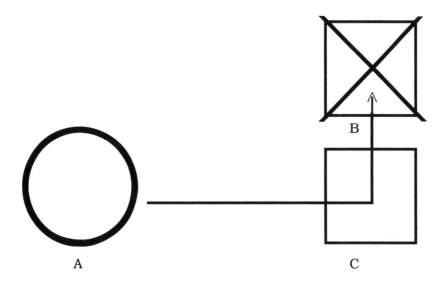

Figure 3. Construct replacement.

In Figure 3 is depicted a situation wherein another person is used as a replacement of the person who has died. This is symbolically represented by how person A has taken the emotions that were invested in person B and prematurely invests them in person C. Construct retention is a means of avoiding the work of grief (see Question and Response on Grief Avoidance Response Styles, pages 115-120); however, it introduces an impossible burden on both the bereaved person and the new person in the relationship.

While the prior relationship remains internalized in the bereaved person, the new person in the relationship often encounters the impossible task of living up to the behavior of the "ghost" that still exists. For healthy new relationships to occur, grief work related to the prior relationship must take place. A specific example of construct replacement can be found on pages 87-108. (Question and Response on Example of Assessment of Complicated Grief Responses).

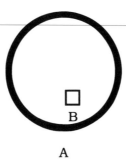

B

A

Figure 4. Construct reconciliation.

In Figure 4 is depicted construct reconciliation wherein the work of mourning has proceeded to a point where a gradual diminishing has occurred of the attachment to the internalized image of the person who has died. The person is still remembered and memorialized; however, no longer has the same claim on the attention or energy of the other. Investment in the internalized image of the other person is weakened to the degree that attachment to new relationships become possible without construct replacement occurring. For a description of criteria for reconciliation, see pages 73-81.

The previous theoretical overview of object relations theory is just that, a theory. We know that any theory applied too rigidly and taken too literally could be misused.

For the reader interested in enhancing his or her knowledge of different conceptual frameworks as to why people grieve the following references are provided:

- Psychodynamic Model[4]

- Illness and Disease Model[5]

- Stress Model[6]

- Sociobiological Model[7]

- Assumptive World Model[8]

- Transcultural Model[9]

REFERENCES

[1] Bowlby, J. (1961). *Attachment and loss, Volume 1.* New York: Basic Books.

[2] Sullender, R.S. (1985). *Grief and growth.* Mahwah, NJ: Paulist Press.

[3] Klein, M. (1960). *Our adult world and its roots in infancy.* London: Tavistock Publications.

[4] Freud, S. (1957). Mourning and Meloncholia. In *Standard edition of complete psychological works of Sigmund Freud,* (Vol. 14). London: Hogarth Press.

[5] Lindemann, E. (1944). Symptomatology and Management of Acute Grief. *American Journal of Psychiatry.*

[6] Caplan, G. (1964). *Principles of preventative psychiatry.* New York: Basic Books.

[7] Averill, J. (1968). Grief: Its Nature and Significance. *Psychological Bulletin, 70,* 721-48.

[8] Parkes, C.M. (1971). Psychosocial Transitions: A Field For Study. *Social Science and Medicine, 5,* 101-15.

[9] Rosenblatt, P.C., Walsh, R.P., & Jackson, D.A. (1976). *Grief and mourning in cross-cultural perspective.* New Haven: HRAF Press.

NOTES

6
UNIQUENESS OF GRIEF RESPONSE

Do people grieve differently, and if so, what factors influence their individual responses?

We have come to understand that each person's grief is uniquely his or her own. As helpers, we only get ourselves into trouble when we try to prescribe what someone's grief experience *should be.*

While society's current interest in learning more about death, dying, and grief is to be applauded, this almost fad-like interest also has created some problems. One such problem is when people around the grieving person adopt a rigid system of beliefs about grief that do not allow for the natural unfolding of the griever's personal experience.

Stage-like thinking about dying and grieving has been appealing to many people. Somehow the "stages of grief" have helped people try to make sense out of an experience that isn't as orderly and predictable as we would like it to be. Attempts have been made to replace fear and lack of understanding with the security that everyone grieves by going through some stages. If only it were so simple!

Just as different people die in different ways, people grieve in different ways. Expecting anything less would be to demonstrate a lack of respect for the uniqueness of the individual person. To think that one's goal as a caregiver is to move people through the stages of grief would be a misuse of counsel. Not every person will experience each and every response described in this text and certainly not necessarily in the order outlined. A variety of thoughts and feelings will be experienced as part of the healing process. For example disorganization, fear, loss, guilt, and anger may or may not occur. Often, regression occurs along the way and invariable some overlapping. Sometimes emotions follow each other within a short period of time; at other times, two or more emotions are present in the grieving person simultaneously. Unfortunately, a person's response to the death of someone loved is never as uncomplicated as described by the written word.

Having acknowledged the importance of understanding the uniqueness of the journey through one's grief, let's review some of the major factors that influence a person's particular response. While ten factors are outlined, they are not intended to be all-inclusive, your awareness of them should prove to enhance your capacity to understand and assist. Following each factor are questions for you as a helper to keep in mind as you enter the helping relationship.

1. The Nature of the Relationship With the Person Who Died.

Different persons will have their own unique responses to the same loss based on the relationship that existed between self and the person that died. For example, with the death of a parent, observers will note that adult children will often grieve in totally different ways. This is only natural based on such influences as the prior attachment in the relationship and the function the relationship served for them. We know for example, that relationships that have had strong components of ambivalence are more difficult to reconcile than those not as conflicted.

Questions To Ask Self As Helper

What was the nature of the relationship that existed between the grieving person and the person that died?

What was the nature of the level of attachment in the relationship?

What functions did the relationship serve in this person's life?

2. The Availability, Helpfulness, and Ability of the Person to Make Use of a Social Support System.

The lack of a consistent, stabilizing support system typically results in a difficult, if not impossible, reconciliation process. To heal in one's grief requires an environment of empathy, support, and encouragement.

On occasion, you will observe a person who would appear to have a support system of family and friends, only to discover that little compassion or support is in the environment. When this is the situation, the person is lacking a vital ingredient that aids in the reconciliation. You also will witness those persons that have support available for a relatively short period of time after the death, only to have this support rapidly dwindle in weeks that follow. Again, for healing to occur, social support must be ongoing.

Some persons do not make effective use of a social support system that is, in fact, available to them. Those persons often isolate themselves and have difficulty accepting others concern and support.

Questions To Ask Self As Helper

Does the person have a positive support system available?

Is this support available on an extended basis? Is the person able and willing to accept support from other persons?

3. The Unique Characteristics of the Bereaved Person.

Previous styles of responding to loss and other crises often are, to some extent, predictive of a person's response to the death of a loved person. If a person has always tried to keep himself/herself distant or run away from crises, he/she may well follow this pattern when confronted with grief. However, if a person has always tended to confront crises head-on and express many thoughts and feelings, he/she will likely follow this pattern of behavior.

Other personality factors such as self-esteem, values, and beliefs also impact on the bereaved person's unique response to grief. Any prior mental health problems also might influence a person's response to loss.

Questions To Ask Self As Helper

How has this person responded to prior loss or crises in his/her lives?

What was this person's personality like prior to the loss, particularly, as it relates to self-esteem?

Any previous history of mental health related difficulties, particularly as it relates to depression?

4. The Unique Characteristics of the Person Who Died.

Just as the characteristics of the bereaved person are reflected in the experience of grief, so too, are the characteristics of the person that died. For example, some person's personalities have been such that he/she has never been very easy to live with. With that person's death, survivors often experience ambivalent feelings. While they may miss the person, often things about the person they do not miss. An illustration of this is when an alcoholic dies. The surviving family may miss the person; however, they are often relieved that they do not have to experience some of the person's behavior.

At the other end of the spectrum is the person whose personality was such that he/she was always a soothing, stabilizing influence within the family. The person managed to "keep the family together." In the absence of the stabilizing force, the surviving family often breaks down and can no longer function in the manner that it once did.

Questions To Ask Self As Helper

What was the personality of the person who died like?

Based on their unique personality, what role did they play within the family, i.e., stabilizer, disrupter, etc.?

5. The Nature of the Death.

The circumstances surrounding the death have a tremendous impact on the survivor's grief. Included among the circumstances of which the helper should be aware are the age of the person that died, an anticipated death versus a sudden death, and any sense of having been able to have prevented the death.

The age of the person that died can have an impact on the psychological acceptance of the death. For example, within the order of the world we anticipate that parents will die before their children. When a child dies it is an assault of the natural course of events. The death of children in our culture is always seen as being untimely. Another example of the impact on age is the 40 year-old person who is thought to be in the "prime of life" that dies.

Numerous studies have addressed the reality that having the opportunity to anticipate a death assists in the griever's adaption to the loss. Sudden, unexpected loss, obviously does not allow the griever any opportunity for psychological preparation.. However, note that having the opportunity to anticipate a death does not lessen one's grief; however, it does provide time to prepare and attempt to understand the reality of the death (see Question and Response on Anticipatory Grief, pages 131-133).

Those persons that have persistent thoughts that they should have been able to have prevented the death typically experience more prolonged and severe grief reactions. While very natural for one to assess one's culpability upon the death of someone loved, some persons continue to blame themselves over a period of time. While a sense of preventatility at times evolves from the griever's own unrealistic perceptions, you will see some persons whose behavior, in fact, could have impacted on the outcome of the death that occurred. One example of this is the person who fell asleep when driving an automobile, with an accident resulting in the death of a passenger.

Questions To Ask Self As Helper

What were the circumstances surrounding the death?

How old was the person that died?

What is the survivor's perception of the timeliness of the death?

Was the death anticipated or was it sudden and unexpected?

Does the person have a persistent sense that they should have been able to have prevented the death?

6. The Person's Religious and Cultural History.

The grieving person's response to death is impacted by unique cultural and religious backgrounds. Different cultures are known for the various ways in which they express or repress their grief. The capacity to respect these differences enhances the helper's effectiveness. Individual differences secondary to religious and cultural backgrounds may assist or detract from the person's journey toward reconciliation of the loss.

Questions To Ask Self As Helper

What is the survivor's religious and cultural background?

How do these backgrounds influence their ability to give themselves permission to mourn?

What can this person teach me about his/her religious and cultural backgrounds?

7. Other Crisis or Stresses in the Person's Life.

An individual loss seldom occurs in isolation. The death of someone loved often means the loss of financial security, the loss of one's long-time friends and perhaps the loss of one's community. The helper should always assess other stresses and losses occurring in the survivor's life. Examples would include, the person who may have some physical disability, strained family or friend relationship, or is unemployed. These additional stresses are known to negatively impact the experiences of one's grief.

Questions To Ask Self As Helper

What other stresses does this person have impacting on their life at this time?

What additional losses have resulted from the death of this person in their life?

8. Previous Experiences With Death.

We now live in what has been termed by sociologist, Robert Fulton, as "the world's first death free generation." This means that it is now possible for a person to grow into adulthood without having experienced a close personal loss. For these persons who have had no previous experience with death, no opportunity has been present to develop resources to cope. In addition, prior negative associations with death can influence one's capacity to grieve in a healthy way. For example, if someone has learned to avoid death and run away from its reality, chances are this pattern will be adopted in the future.

Question To Ask Self As Helper

What is the survivor's previous experiences with death?

How have these previous experiences influenced their attitudes and behaviors related to grief?

9. The Social Expectations Based on the Sex of the Survivor.

This relates to how males and females are taught differently about expressing their feelings. Generally men are encouraged to "be strong" and restrain themselves from the expression of painful emotions. Typically, men have more difficulty in allowing themselves to be helpless than women do. Women often experience difficulty in expressing feelings of anger; whereas, men tend to be more quick to express explosive emotions. The key here is to respect the ways the person has been socialized based on sex, to respond in the face of loss in their lives. The task of the helper is not to change their response, but to understand it and facilitate its healthy expression.

Question To Ask Self As Helper

How has this person been socially influenced to respond to loss based on his/her sex?

10. The Ritual or Funeral Experience.

Decisions survivors make related to the experience of the funeral can either help or hinder the journey through grief. In spite of frequent criticism, funerals assist in both social and psychological reconciliation after a death. Numerous research findings have confirmed the value of the funeral. Many people who experience complicated grief, relate that their experience with the funeral was minimized or inadequate in some way.

The funeral can serve as a time to honor the person who has died, bring survivors close together for needed support, affirm that life goes on, and give mourners a context of meaning related to their own religious or philosophical backgrounds. If the purpose of the funeral is minimized or distorted in some way, the experience of reconciling one's grief often becomes more difficult (see Question and Response on Funeral Ritual pages 145-150)

Questions To Ask Self As Helper

What was this person's experience with the funeral?

Did the funeral experience aid in the expression or repression of their grief?

What role does this person believe the funeral played in his/her experience with grief?

Again, keeping the above factors in mind will aid you in understanding the person's unique experience with grief. On occasion, you may find it helpful to review these influences, as well as, those questions to ask yourself as a helper.

7
OVERVIEW OF NORMAL EXPERIENCE OF GRIEF

Would you please provide an overview of your understanding of the normal experience of grief and provide some guidelines regarding the helper's role at this time?

Common Dimensions of Normal Grief

This section of the book provides an overview of the normal adult grief process. First, let's remind ourselves that grief is a privilege that comes with the capacity to give and receive love. The work of grief is a natural process by which the emotions reorganize themselves to cope with the loss and re-establish healthy relationships.

The previous section reinforced the importance of acknowledging the uniqueness of the mourner's response and noted that grief does not conform to a certain time frame, nor is its expression limited to definite thoughts, feelings and behaviors. This precludes a view of the experience of grief as one in which any specific individual will follow a definitely prescribed pattern.

A vital task of the helper is to become familiar with those thoughts, feelings, and behaviors that may be expressed by the person who is grieving. Then, being aware of those experiences, to become capable of responding in ways that assist the person in movement toward reconciliation.

A number of observers have defined models of grief that are often referred to as "stages" (e.g., Bowlby[1], Engel[2], Kubler-Ross[3], Lindemann[4], Parkes[5]). Erich Lendemann's 1944 article on the symptomatology and management of grief was one of the first writings in this area. His observations were based on interviews with over 100 grieving persons who had experienced the death of family members in Boston's Coconut Grove restaurant fire. Lindemann and other authors most typically describe stages as moving from disorganization to reorganization or as moving from shock to recovery.

My goal for the purposes of this text is to present a multi-dimensional model of an adult's grief experience based upon my personal experiences with loss, clinical experiences with grieving persons, and teachings from the literature. In Figure 5 is provided an outline of the model we will explore here. Please note that three broad classifications of grief, titled EVASION, ENCOUNTER, AND RECONCILIATION are provided along with a more detailed description of components of these experiences. By no means do I pretend that this model is all-inclusive; however, I do hope it aids in the clergyperson's helping efforts.

Not every person will experience each and every response described and certainly not necessarily in the order outlined. Some regression will occur along the way and invariable some over-lapping. Unfortunately, as previously written, a person's response to loss is never as uncomplicated as described by the written word. You will note that the word "dimension" of grief, as opposed to "stage" of grief is used in an effort to prevent thinking that the experience of grief occurs in some kind of ordered fashion.

Prior to highlighting what we will term dimensions of the grief experience, I think it will be helpful to briefly highlight the concept of *Tasks of Mourning.* Worden[6] made an excellent distinction between the experiences of grief and the tasks of mourning. He outlined how the experience of phases or stages of grief imply a certain passivity; whereas, tasks of mourning imply that the mourner needs to take action and can do something. This concept of tasks can help the mourner realize that grief is not something to simply experience, but that, in fact he or she can do something to aid in the healing process. A review of reconciliation needs/tasks of the mourner are provided on pages 73-81 of this text.

Now, keeping in mind the uniqueness of each person's experience with grief, let's familiarize ourselves with some of the more common dimensions of the experience.

	EVASION From the new reality	ENCOUNTER with the new reality	RECONCILIATION to the new reality
Mourning Characteristics	Shock Denial Numbness Disbelief	Disorganization Confusion, Searching, Yearning Generalized Anxiety Panic, Fear Physiological Changes Explosive Emotions Guilt, Remorse Assessing Culpability Loss, Emptiness Sadness Relief, Release	The capacity to organize and plan one's life toward the future The establishment of new and healthy relationships The capacity to being open to more change in one's life.
Primary Needs of Mourner	Self protection Psychological Shock Absorber	To experience and express reality of the death To tolerate the emotional suffering	To convert relationship with deceased person to one of memory To develop a new self-identity To relate the loss to context of meaning
Time Course (specific information difficult to predict)	Weeks, potentially months (variable)	Many months (variable)	Twenty-four to thirty-six months (variable)
Primary Role of Helper	Supportive presence Assist with practical matters	Encourage expression of thoughts, feelings Stabilizing, comforting presence	Supportive encouragement Understanding, available presence

Figure 5. Dimensions of grief: A model for understanding

SHOCK/DENIAL/NUMBNESS/DISBELIEF

The constellation of experiences of shock, denial, numbness, and disbelief are often nature's way of temporarily protecting the mourner from the reality of the death of someone loved. In reflecting on this experience, most mourners make comments like "I was there, but yet I really wasn't," "It was like a dream," "I managed to do what needed to be done, but I didn't feel a part of it." Reports of feeling dazed and stunned are very common during this time.

When little, if any, opportunity was available to anticipate a death, this constellation of experiences is typically heightened and prolonged. However, even when the death of someone loved is expected, we often see components of shock, denial, numbness, and disbelief. This experience creates an insulation from the reality of the death until one is more able to tolerate what one doesn't want to believe. It serves as a "temporary time-out" or "psychological shock absorber." Our emotions need time to catch up with what our minds have been told. At one level, the mourner knows the person is dead, yet is not able or willing to believe it. As previously written, in terms of object relation theory, this is when construct retention occurs.

Often people do not remember specific words that are spoken to them during this period of time. The mind is blocking and is not connected to listening. However, people do remember how they were made to feel by those around them. Obviously this tells us something very important about what to do and not to do at this time. This will be discussed under the heading "Clergyperson's Helping Role."

This constellation of experiences acts as an anesthetic; the pain is there, but one does not experience it in its full reality. In a very real sense the body and mind take over in an effort to help the person survive. Typically a physiological component accompanies this experience that includes a take over by the autonomic nervous system. Heart palpitations, queasiness, stomach pain, and dizziness are among the most common experiences.

A wide spectrum of what might be termed bizarre behaviors in other contexts is often observed. Hysterical crying, outbursts of anger, laughing, and fainting are frequently witnessed at this time. In actuality, expressing these behaviors allows for survival.

Unfortunately, people around mourners at this time will often try to suppress these experiences. Many of you as clergy can probably recount experiences of being called in to "quiet the griever."

This dimension of the grief experience typically reflects only the beginning of the person's journey through grief. However, important to note is that many people, both lay and professionals, acknowledge these manifestations as the entire mourning process. This phenomenon is reflected in the often heard comment from the bereaved person: "People were there for me right at the time of the death and for a short time thereafter, but they quickly returned to their routines and seemed to forget about me and my need for support and understanding." These kinds of statements tell helpers something very important about not only being available at the time of the death, but for a long time thereafter.

The process of beginning to embrace the full reality of the death and move beyond this dimension of one's grief varies widely. Shock and numbness wane only at the pace one is able and ready to acknowledge feelings of loss. To provide a specific time frame for everyone would be to over generalize. However, based on my personal experiences, clinical experiences, and knowledge of the literature, this spectrum of experiences frequently is most intense during the first four to six week period immediately following the death of someone loved.

However, even after one becomes capable of embracing the reality of the loss, sometimes this dimension still comes to the surface. This particularly is seen at such times as the anniversary of death or other special occasions (birthdays, holidays, etc.). I also have repeatedly witnessed the resurgence of this dimension when the person visits a place associated with a special memory of the dead person (see Question and Response on Anniversary Reactions page 113-114).

In actuality, the person's mind approaches and retreats from the reality of a death over and over again, as he or she tries to embrace and integrate the meaning of the death into his or her life. The availability of the consistent support system allows this process to occur. During this process of acknowledging one's grief, at times the hope still is that one will wake-up from a bad dream and that none of this really happened.

Clergyperson's Helping Role. Critical to the helping role at this time is to acknowledge that shock, denial, numbness, and disbelief is not something to be discouraged, but, instead, something to be understood and allowed. To do anything else would be an attempt to take a person's grief away from him or her. A significant amount of the mourner's natural behavior during this dimension results in attempts to have other people care for him or her at a time when the person is unable to do so.

In my experiences, the primary task of the helper at this time, is to simply "be with" the person. Remember, we are aware that people do not, at this time, remember specific words that are said to them but do remember how they are made to feel by those around them. Quiet, caring, supportive companionship often becomes the person's greatest need at this time. The art of being physically and emotionally present, while at the same time not invading the person's space is not always an easy task. When we as helpers feel helpless, often our first inclination is to talk too much. Becoming capable of acknowledging our own feelings of helplessness at this time allows us to become more effective in our caregiving. In acknowledging our helplessness, we can recognize that bombarding the person with words only serves to disorient the person further.

We also might tend to want to do and say what the person may need and want to do and say at this time. Given time and support, the mourner finds value in doing and saying for himself or herself. This allows the person to begin the work of grief. Again, prevent yourself from taking this opportunity away from the individual. Of course, performing many practical things for the person (like seeing that meals are prepared for them) will be much appreciated. The major point being, don't do for the person what he or she wants to do for self.

Related to the previous statements is the awareness that during this time the mourner will often demonstrate a natural difficulty with decision making and anything that requires concentration. As an effective helper, do not collaborate with others who may be attempting to force decisions out of the person. If well intentioned people are pushing for decisions, you can become an advocate for a waiting period. Decisions can and should be temporarily postponed until the person feels capable of participating in the decision making process.

When at all possible, a quiet, physical environment should be provided to the grieving person at this time. When in shock, people become more disoriented when bombarded with outside noise. In a strange way quietness becomes comforting. Providing a blanket for warmth and a hot drink are also helpful to many people at this time.

Find out who the person may want to have with him or her at this time and don't become offended when that person is not you. On some occasions when a person who has not had any previous relationship with you, your presence, in fact, may be resented. If this is the situation, simply find out who the person wants and try to see that that person becomes available. On other occasions, even when you have not had a prior relationship with a person, you will sense that he or she finds comfort in your presence. Sometimes this is because you are a clergyperson and represent faith and at other times this may be that you are a fellow human being.

Use the person's reaction to you as a guide for your own behavior. Be careful not to project your own needs into the situation. I once heard said that perhaps the most effective helping role at this time is: "Mouths closed, ears open, and presence available." Perhaps keeping this in mind as an underlying theme will assist you as you reach out to comfort at this most difficult time. (For discussion of the helper's role related to encouraging the expression of emotions and respecting denial see page 121-122.)

DISORGANIZATION/CONFUSION/SEARCHING/YEARNING

Often, the most isolating and frightening part of the experience of grief begins after the funeral. This is frequently when the mourner begins to be confronted with the reality of the death. As one woman expressed, "I felt as if I was a lonely traveler with no companion, and worse yet, no destination. It was as if I couldn't find myself or anybody else."

This is when many people experience the "going crazy syndrome." Because normal thoughts and behaviors in grief are so different from what one normally experiences, then only naturally does the grieving person not know whether the behavior is normal or abnormal. Those experiences described in the next paragraph are so common after the death of someone loved that they must be acknowledged as part of the normal process of mourning. A major task of the helper is to assist in normalizing these experiences.

Often present is a sense of restlessness, agitation, impatience, and ongoing confusion. An analogy that seems to fit is that it is like being in the middle of a wild, rushing river, whereby you can't get a grasp on anything. Disconnected thoughts race through the mourner's mind and strong emotions at times are overwhelming. Disorganization and confusion often manifests themselves in terms of an inability to complete any tasks. A project may get started but go unfinished. Time is distorted and seen as something to be endured. Certain times of day, often early morning and late night, are times when the person feels most disoriented and confused. Disorganization and confusion are often accompanied by fatigue and lack of initiative. The acute pain of the loss is devastating to the point normal pleasures do not seem to matter.

A restless searching for the person who died is a common part of the experience. Parkes, Bowlby, and others have written extensively about searching behavior. Yearning for the dead person and being preoccupied with memories of them lead to intense moments of distress. Often a shift in perception makes other people look like the dead person. A phenomenon sometimes exists whereby sounds are interpreted as signals that the person has returned. For example, hearing the garage door open and the person entering the house as that person had done for so many years.

Visual hallucinations occur so frequently that they cannot be considered abnormal. I personally prefer the term "memory picture" to visual hallucination. Seemingly as part of the searching and yearning process the mourner not only experiences a sense of the dead person's presence, but may have transient experiences of looking across the room and seeing the person.

Other common features during this time, are difficulties with eating and sleeping. Many people experience loss of appetite while others overeat. Those people who do eat often note a lack of being able to taste their food. Difficulty in going to sleep and early morning awakening also are common experiences.

Dreams about the dead person are often a part of the experience at this time. Dreams are often an unconscious means of searching for the person who has died. It is often described to me by people as an opportunity to be close to the person. As one widower related, "I don't seem to have any control over it, but each night I find myself dreaming about my wife. I see us together, happy and content. If it only could be that way again." The content of these dreams often reflects the real life changes in the person's experience with mourning.

Clergyperson's Helping Role. During this complex dimension of grief, the person tends to worry about the normalcy of the experience. Thus, the mourner is not only faced with the pain of the grief, but also the fear that he or she may be "going crazy." Reassurance and education about the normalcy of the experience allows the person to share thoughts, feelings, and behaviors outside of self.

As previously written, grief must be shared outside of oneself for healing to occur. The helper must be patient and attentive as the person tells the story over and over. Repetition occurs with what the person shares with you as the person works to internalize and reconcile self to the death that has occurred.

During this time, the mourner will sense your genuine interest in listening and attempting to understand. The person will not share the grief with you if he or she does not feel an open willingness to listen and understand being generated from you.

The means to move from disorganization toward reconciliation is through the expression of thoughts and feelings. The person may need to talk and cry for long periods of time. The role of the helper is not to interrupt with reasoning, but to let crying and talking take their natural course.

The thoughts, feelings, and behaviors of this dimension do not come all at once and are often experienced in a wave-like fashion. The mourner needs to be supported through each wave and reassured that the surges do not mean regression but are a normal part of the experience of grief. At times, the content of what the person might be saying could make little sense; however, this can be helpful and clarifying for the person.

During this time, the mourner should be actively discouraged from making critical decisions like selling the home and moving to another community. With the judgement making difficulties that naturally come with this part of the experience, ill-timed decisions can often result in secondary losses.

GENERALIZED ANXIETY/PANIC/FEAR

Feelings of anxiety, panic, and fear are often experienced by the mourner. These feelings are typically generated from thought such as : "Will my life have any purpose without this person? I don't think I can live without him." The death of someone loved, naturally threatens one's feelings of security and results in the evolution of anxiety.

As the person's mind is continually brought back to the pain of loss, panic may set in. Anxiety and fear often relates to thoughts about "going crazy." The thought of being abnormal creates even more intense fear.

Fear of what the future holds; fear that one person's death will result in others; increased awareness of one's own mortality; feelings of vulnerability about being able to survive without the person; inability to concentrate; and emotional and physical fatigue all serve to heighten anxiety, panic, and fear. The mourner often feels overwhelmed by everyday problems and concerns. To make matters worse, a change may occur in economic status, large bills may need to be paid, and the fear often increases of becoming dependent on others.

Clergyperson's Helping Role. The major helping principal to keep in mind regarding anxiety, panic, and fear is the need to explore supportively and to acknowledge these experiences within the mourner. Not talking about fears only results in them growing larger. Often a helpful procedure is to communicate your willingness to discuss fears by providing an open-ended opportunity such as "people have taught me that with the death of someone loved, there are often fears that arise. Have you had any fears to come about within you?" Then, follow the person's lead as they begin to explore those fears. Again, support the naturalness of those fears and express your willingness to be a sounding board for their expression. Your awareness of the common fears outlined in this section will assist you in anticipating some of what might be shared.

PHYSIOLOGICAL CHANGES

A person's body responds to what the mind has been told at a time of acute grief. Some of the most common physiological changes that the mourner may experience are as follows:

Generalized lack of energy and fatigue
Shortness of breath
Feelings of emptiness in the stomach
Tightness in the throat and chest
Sensitivity to noise
Heart palpitations
Queasiness
Difficulty in sleeping or on other occasions prolonged sleeping
Headaches
Agitation and generalized tension

With loss, the mourner's immune system breaks down and he or she becomes more vulnerable to illness. Many studies have documented significant increases in illness following bereavement (see Question and Response on Morbidity and Mortality following Bereavement on pages 83-85).

In the majority of instances, physical symptoms are normal and temporary. At times, the mourner will unconsciously assume a "sick role" in an effort to legitimize his or her feelings to others. This often results in frequent visits to the physician. Unfortunately, assumption of the "sick role" often occurs when the person does not receive encouragement to mourn, or, doesn't give self permission to express thoughts and feelings in other ways.

Clergyperson's Helping Role. When little or no outlet exists to express feelings in a natural way, the person expresses feelings through his or her physical being. As a caregiver you also should be aware that physical disorders present prior to the loss tend to become worse. In addition, often what occurs is a transient identification with the physical symptoms that have caused the death of the person loved. For example, if the spouse dies of a heart attack, the person may complain of chest pains.

Dependent on the extent of the symptoms, suggesting that the person consult a physician is appropriate to rule out physical causes for the symptoms. Every person who is seen at the Center For Loss and Life Transition is referred for a general medical examination. Helping the person understand physical symptoms as a normal facet of grief often allows these symptoms to lessen as the work of grief progresses.

EXPLOSIVE EMOTIONS

Because of society's attitude toward anger, this dimension of explosive emotions is often the most upsetting to those persons around the griever. Often, both the mourner and those persons trying to be supportive to the mourner have problems acknowledging and creating an environment for the expression of this wide spectrum of emotions. The reason for this is frequently related to the uncertainty of how to respond to the griever at this time.

We sometimes oversimplify these emotions by talking only about anger. The mourner also may experience feelings of hate, blame, terror, resentment, rage, and jealousy. While these emotions all have their distinctive features, adequate similarities exist in the person's underlying needs to warrant discussing the various explosive emotions together. Beneath the explosive emotions are the griever's more primary feelings of pain, helplessness, frustration, fear, and hurt.

Expression of explosive emotions often relates to a desire to restore things to the way they were before the death. Even though a conscious awareness is present that the person has died the need to express explosive emotions and a desire to "get the person back" seems to be grounded in psychobiological roots. As John Bowlby[7] has observed:

> There are therefore good biological reasons for every separation to be responded to in an automatic instinctive way with aggressive behavior; irretrievable loss is statistically so unusual that it is not taken into account. In the course of our evolution, it appears our instinctual equipment has come to be so fashioned that all losses are assumed to be retrievable and are responded to accordingly. (pp. 317)

So while the expression of explosive emotions does not create the desired result of bringing the dead back to life, we can hopefully understand the naturalness of its existence. If viewed in this fashion, anger and other related emotions can be seen as an intelligent response that the grieving person is making to restore the relationship that has been lost. Actually, in my experience, a healthy survival value occurs in being able to temporarily protest the painful reality of the loss. It's as if having the capacity to express anger gives one the courage to survive at this particular point in time. The griever who either does not give self the permission, or doesn't receive the permission from others to protest, may slide into a chronic depressive response that includes no desire to go on living.

The fact that the dead person does not come back despite the griever's explosive emotions is part of the reality testing needed for the eventual process of reconciliation. With the gradual awareness that the person who has died will, in fact, not return, the need for the expression of these emotions changes over time. Only when the reality that the loss is permanent creeps in does the person free him or herself from this task of grieving. Should the explosive emotions become chronic, not changing over time, this would be an indication of a complicated grief response.

Let's look at some of the ways these emotions are expressed—

Explosive emotions basically have two avenues for expression: outward or inward. What the griever does with these emotions can have a powerful impact on the journey through the grief. The anger may be expressed outwardly toward friends and family, the physician, God, the person who died, the clergyperson, people who have not experienced loss, or any number of other persons or places.

For our present purposes, let's briefly expand on anger that gets directed toward God. Some mourners perceive death to be a form of punishment and naturally respond with anger toward those they feel are responsible for the death. God, seen as having power over life and death becomes a target for the expression of explosive emotions. For example, a protestant man remarked: "I stopped attending church after my wife's death. She and I had been so devoted in our faith and yet He took her from me. I don't see any point in being faithful to Him if He is not going to be faithful to me."

Clergypersons have taught me that they often feel the most helpless in the face of mourners expressing anger toward God. At times, the sense of a need to defend God is felt. And yet, God, in his natural "whipping post" position probably doesn't need anyone to defend Him. As we all realize, He has been taking pretty good care of Himself for some time now. I also would mention that having anger at God speaks of having a relationship with God. If no relationship exists the person would probably not feel anger.

Experience suggests that as soon as you begin to defend God, you may dig yourself a hole that is difficult to get out of. Frequently, the more you defend your position that the person should not be angry at God, the more the person strives to convince you that they should—your response causes the person to defend their response.

Anger toward God is not something to be judged, but instead, is something to be understood in the context of the person's phenomenological experience. If you are able to fight any felt sense of need to defend God, you can often enter into a dialogue with the person that allows him or her to grow through the grief. The person already feels abandoned by God, certainly he or she doesn't need to be abandoned by you in your role of supportive helper.

As previously mentioned, another frequent target for the expression of anger is family members. In a study of the first year of bereavement, Glick, Weiss, and Parkes[8] noted that widows were angry at family members for lack of support, for over protection, and for disappointment in expected help from relatives. Among other things, anger also was reported over funeral details, withdrawal, and at the eagerness of relatives to acquire possessions of the person who died.

In some instances, mourners will direct the anger inward resulting in low self-esteem, depression, chronic feelings of guilt, physical complaints, and potentially suicide. When anger is repressed and directed inward, the person's experience with grief often becomes complicated and chronic. Anger turned inward may result in agitation, tension, and general restlessness. It is as if something is inside the person trying to get out. Should you observe cues that lead you to believe that the mourner has turned his or her anger inward, an appropriate procedure might be to refer the person to someone more experienced in counseling the bereaved.

Clergyperson's Helping Role. Not all mourners experience the same depth of explosive emotions. However, the majority of people with whom you come in contact who have experienced the death of someone in their life will be able to relate to some of the experiences outlined in the proceeding paragraphs. Therefore, in your helping role you will want to validate these emotions when expressed and explore them with the mourner when he or she does not.

A word of caution: obviously, you *do not want to prescribe* these feelings but be alert for them. The majority of studies on mourning have focused on premature and unexpected deaths where explosive emotions are very commonly seen. However, in some situations where a death is more anticipated, explosive emotions may be mild or not exist at all.

Ultimately, healthy grief requires that explosive emotions, when present, be expressed not repressed. Many grieving people need a supportive listener who can tolerate, encourage, and validate explosive emotions without judging, retaliating, or arguing. The comforting presence of a caring helper often allows the person to let go of pent-up emotions.

Keep in mind that as a member of the helping profession you may well be rebuffed by those very persons you would like to help. Anger can be directed toward people who attempt to comfort, because for the mourner, accepting comfort is too acknowledge the pain of the loss that has occurred.

Hostility directed toward helpers is certainly understandable. For example, if we as helpers are aware that one of the tasks of mourning is to acknowledge the reality of the loss we naturally want to assist the person in confronting this reality. However, at certain points in grief for some people, they are not seeking confrontation with reality, they are seeking reunion with the person who has died. So, the helper who does not take sides in the mourner's struggle between striving for reunion and acknowledging the painful reality of the loss proves to be very therapeutic. This is a delicate helping task whereby you are not encouraging denial, but communicating an understanding of the search for reunion. The helper who does not achieve this balance is often met with angry feelings on the part of the mourner.

For the mourner who expresses explosive emotions toward the person who died, an important procedure is to help the mourner achieve balance between both negative and positive feelings. I have seen a number of people in counseling who will become rigidly focused on negative feelings toward the deceased as a means of preventing self from acknowledging the hurt, pain, and sadness associated with the loss. Assisting the person to achieve the appropriate balance relates to the art of helping.

As you strive to aid persons in this dimension of grief, keep in mind the underlying feelings of pain, helplessness, frustration, fear, and hurt. The helper needs to be in touch with these primary feelings, and at the same time listen permissively and accept all other feelings. Through permissive listening and responsive guidance, the griever learns that his or her feelings are neither good nor bad, but are merely his or hers and are present. A real need at this point is for the helper to be accepting of all feelings and to support the griever as such strong and strange feelings change over time.

So, we have come to understand that anger and other explosive emotions in grief can be natural and healthy. While anger will at times express itself in irrational ways, friends, family, and helpers who fail to realize this can leave the griever feeling abandoned, guilty, and confused over experiencing anger.

In reality, explosive emotions cannot and should not be prevented from being expressed. The difficulty is not the presence of these emotions, but finding and giving oneself permission to be angry. When faced with explosive emotions the mourner is most in need of stabilizing, sustaining relationships. As a helper, you have the opportunity and privilege of creating just such a relationship.

GUILT/REMORSE/ASSESSING CULPABILITY

We now recognize that guilt and self-blame are often seen in the grieving person. A natural process of assessing one's culpability seems to occur following loss through death. Some people become obsessed by guilt, leading to a complicated grief response and the need for specialized help, while others come to understand the normalcy of temporary feelings of guilt.

Guilt evolves in a number of ways as a part of the experience of grief. Perhaps the most common is the "If only I would have..." or "Why didn't I..." syndrome. This often relates to a sense of wanting to change the circumstances surrounding the death or unfinished business in the relationship with the person who died.

Some examples of common "if onlys" that you may hear the person express are as follows:

"If only I would have known he was dying."
"If only I would have gotten her to the doctor sooner."
"If only I insisted she take better care of herself."
"If only I had been a better wife."

These are only a few, of hundreds of examples that could be given. While the expression of guilt is often not logical or real, it is still a natural part of the healing process. Unfortunately, as helpers, we often find ourselves wanting to rush in and try to take the person's need to express guilt or self-blame away. We will explore this more in our discussion of the helper's role.

Feelings of guilt are often expressed about those days or weeks just prior to the death of the person. Assessing one's culpability during this time often seems to be an indirect means of assuring oneself that they did everything that could have been done for the person. This is most certainly an understandable need on the part of the survivor. A common theme I often witness at this time is a desire to have created opportunities to talk with the person about his or her dying. For example, "If only we could have been honest with each other about what was happening."

Surviving a person who has died often generates feelings of guilt. Survival guilt leads the person to ask "How is it that he/she died and I survived? I recently saw a middle-aged man in counseling that had been driving an automobile in which his wife was a passenger. He fell asleep at the wheel and an accident occurred. His wife died instantly and he walked away without a scratch. He needed to be able to explore the question of his survival in the face of her death. In his mind, his sense of responsibility for falling asleep demanded his death, but certainly not his wife's.

Another type of guilt evolves when a person's death brings some sense of relief or release. This often occurs when the person who died had been ill for a prolonged period of time or the relationship was conflicted. In the case of a long illness, the mourner may not miss the frequent trips to the hospital or the physical responsibilities of caring for the person. If the person is not able to acknowledge this sense of relief as natural, and not equal to a lack of love, they may feel guilty for feeling relieved.

An example of the relief-guilt syndrome in a conflicted relationship is as follows: I have worked with a number of families who have experienced the death of an alcoholic member of the family. Upon the person's death, naturally certain behaviors are no longer within the family. Again, if the survivors are able to be understanding of their sense of relief, all is well and good. However, they often get caught in the trap of the relief-guilt syndrome.

Another form of guilt is that which evolves from long-standing personality factors of the survivor. Some people are taught early in life, typically during childhood, that they are responsible when anything bad or unfortunate occurs. When a death occurs in their life the first place they look to find blame is at themselves. Obviously, this kind of guilt relates to long standing personality factors that would have to be something on which to work in the context of the counseling relationship.

Guilt also can be experienced when the mourner begins to re-experience any kind of joy or happiness in his or her life. This often related to loyalty to the deceased and fears that being happy in some way betrays the relationship that once was. Opportunities to explore these feelings are often necessary as the person moves forward in the experience of the grief.

We often witness feelings of guilt when the survivor was not able to be present when the death occurred. Often the irrational, yet understandable thought is that, "If I had been there, the person would not have died." This often relates to a desire to have power or control over something which one has no power or control over. After all, if I feel guilty, it means I could have done something to change the outcome of what happened. The survivors thinking that if they were present, the outcome would have been different seems to be an attempt to counter a felt sense of helplessness and impotence. Again, certainly an understandable response in the context of the painful reality of the loss.

You also will witness occasions when feelings of guilt will be induced by those persons around the griever. This often occurs through ignorance, lack of understanding, or the need to project outside of oneself onto others. Projecting outside of oneself is illustrated by family members who, in wanting to deny their own pain and any sense of culpability, strike-out against other family members.

An unfortunate example of guilt induction is the family friend who informs the recently bereaved widow: "Your husband would not have died if you had had a closer relationship with God." These kinds of messages often become very destructive to the mourner who is already struggling with grief.

People sometimes feel guilty for having had a conscious or unconscious wish for the death toward the person who has died. This relates to the concept of magical thinking that somehow one's thoughts can cause action. The majority of relationships have components of ambivalence whereby a person will think on occasion: "I wish you would go away and leave me alone." Or, in highly conflicted relationships an even more direct thought of wanting the relationship to end. When the person does die, the survivor has a sense that he or she somehow caused the death.

While all relationships have periods of time when negative thoughts are experienced, obviously, one's mind does not have the power to inflict death on someone. Again however, you can easily see how the person might connect thoughts with events that occur.

Feelings of guilt are not limited to any select group of people. They are a natural part of the experience of grief. Being aware of the normalcy of guilt and the need to assess culpability hopefully allows you to enter the helping relationship with an open mind and an available presence.

Clergyperson's Helping Role. In relation to this dimension of grief, one of the helper's primary roles is one of permissive, patient, and non-judgmental listener. This allows the mourner the opportunity to explore feelings of guilt and opens awareness for rebuilding.

Try to avoid the natural urge to quickly and prematurely explain the person's guilt away. Doing so won't work and we simply cannot do for the person what one must do for oneself. However, you can provide a stabilizing presence that allows the mourner to assess culpability. Only in exploring what one should or should not feel guilty about does the mourner come to some understanding of what the limits of the responsibility are.

Provide opportunities for the mourner to talk about the circumstances surrounding the death. You then can do some reality testing with the person. For example, the mourner says, "I think I should have been of more help to him during his long illness." You might respond with, "Help me understand what you did to be of help." The person then goes on to relate what they did do to be of help to the person. Again, you are not judging whether they should have done more or less, but assisting them in coming to one's own conclusions.

Of course, such a thing as legitimate guilt can occur wherein the person can identify some things they genuinely could have done differently in the relationship with the person that died. The art of helping this person becomes more difficult. As helpers we all tend to have our own unique ways of working to assist people with legitimate guilt. Our religious and philosophical backgrounds play a part in what we see as both therapeutic and appropriate. I can only share with you what I tend to do under these circumstances, realizing that what you do may be very different, yet effective.

Typically, I attempt to work within the mourners' own frame of references to what they believe they need to do with their legitimate guilt. I find that many people from religious backgrounds find value in confession to God and asking for forgiveness. While this doesn't fit for everyone, it does seem to fit many.

The process may go something like this: The person teaches me about his or her religious frame of reference and I sense the mourner's need to ask for forgiveness. This leads to a discussion of the process of atonement (theologically, the word for taking care of guilt). I ask what is felt as being needed to be done related to atonement. The person tells me and we then map out a plan within the individual's frame of reference to seek atonement.

For example, a man in his sixties once shared with me that he had previously physically abused his wife who years later died of cancer. He was of Catholic faith and taught me about his need to be forgiven from his theological perspective. The decision was made that he would ask for God's forgiveness and confess his admitted wrong doing to his priest. This began a process for him of (1) seeking God's forgiveness, (2) acknowledging to himself and others what he had done wrong, (3) accepting that what had happened had happened, (4) allowing himself to forgive himself in the eyes of his God, and (5) create an environment for him to more fully mourn his wife's death. Through exploration of his guilt this man was able to restore a lost relationship with God, and with himself. Obviously, this is only one example and helping people with guilt is often as unique as the person and the surrounding circumstances.

As a helper you also will want to be alert to the person's conscious need to punish self secondary to feelings of guilt. Self-punishment is illustrated through chronic physical complaints, chronic depression, inappropriate risk-taking, self-defeating relationship choices, and general neglect of one's own well-being. These are signs and symptoms of complicated grief that require referral for specialized help.

We must acknowledge that guilt can, and often is, a component of complicated grief, particularly chronic depression, and cannot be ignored. Guilt is one of the most frequent emotional realms in which people become trapped and have difficulties. One of the worst things the mourner can do is ignore and repress feelings of guilt, because we know the many emotional and physical problems will evolve when this occurs.

Should you note themes of unresolved and persistent guilt, you should probably consider consultation with another professional or someone who specializes in loss counseling. Depressive and self-destructive guilt can become dangerous when it goes unattended. However, in the majority of instances, you will find yourself competent to be with the person as he or she explores feelings of guilt.

LOSS/EMPTINESS/SADNESS

With good reason, this constellation of feelings and experiences is often the most difficult for the griever. The full sense of loss never occurs all at once. Weeks, more often months pass after the death before the person is confronted by how much his or her life is changed by the loss. A person that has been a vital part of one's life is no longer present. The mourner certainly has the right to have feelings of loss, emptiness, and sadness. Unfortunately, many people surrounding the mourner frequently try to take these feelings away. Friends, family, and sometimes even professional caregivers erroneously believe that their job is to distract the mourner from these feelings.

At times the grieving person has intense feelings of loss and loneliness. When these experiences initially occur, they are usually very frightening to the person. Thinking and hoping that they have already experienced the most devastating of emotions, they are usually unprepared for the depth of this experience.

Given the opportunity, the majority of mourners will share that the following times are among the most difficult: weekends; holidays; upon initially waking in the morning; late at night, particularly at bedtime; family meal times; upon arriving home to an empty house; and any kind of anniversary occasion. These difficult times usually have some special connection to the person who has died.

Loss, emptiness, and sadness may be intense enough to be considered depression. Much debate is in the literature on grief concerning the distinction between grief and depression. Grief is accompanied by many symptoms of depression such as: sleep disturbance, appetite disturbance, decreased energy, withdrawal, guilt, dependency, lack of concentration, and a sense of losing control. Changes in one's normal capacity to function along with these and other depressive symptoms often result in the griever feeling isolated, helpless, and child-like. This normal regression that accompanies grief naturally impacts on one's sense of esteem and well-being. The person often needs help understanding that these characteristics of mourning are temporary and will change over time.

An important procedure is to note some differences between the normal depressive experience of grief and clinical depression. Recognizing that other caregivers may use other criteria, the following are some of the distinctions I find helpful to distinguish between depressive grief and other forms of depression.

Normal Grief	Clinical Depression
Responds to comfort and support	Does not accept support
Often openly angry	Irritable and may complain but does not directly express anger
Relates depressed feelings to loss experienced	Does not relate experiences to a particular life event
Can still experience moments of enjoyment in life	Exhibits an all pervading sense of doom
Exhibits feelings of sadness and emptiness	Projects a sense of hopelessness and chronic emptiness
May have transient physical complaints	Has chronic physical complaints
Expresses guilt over some specific aspect of the loss	Has generalized feelings of guilt
Has temporary impact upon self-esteem	Presents a deep loss of esteem

Figure 6. Possible distinctions between depressive grief and other forms of depression.

In normal grief, the person responds to comfort and support; whereas, depressives often do not accept support. The bereaved are often openly angry; whereas, the depressive complains and is irritable but does not directly express anger. Bereaved persons can relate their depressed features to the loss they have experienced; whereas, depressives often do not relate their experience to any life event. In normal grief, people can still experience moments of enjoyment in life; whereas, with the depressive an all pervading sense of doom exists. Those people around the griever can sense feelings of sadness and emptiness; whereas, depressives project a sense of hopelessness and chronic emptiness. The griever is more likely to have transient physical complaints; whereas, the depressive has chronic physical complaints. The griever often expresses guilt over some specific aspect of the loss; whereas, the depressive often has generalized feelings of guilt. While the self-esteem of the griever is temporarily impacted upon, it is not the depth of loss of esteem usually observed in the depressive. See Figure 6.

Obviously, it is not always easy to distinguish between the depression of grief and clinical forms of depressive illness. If you should find yourself in doubt regarding a differential diagnosis between the two, a wise procedure is to consider consultation from other trained professionals. On those occasions where loss precipitates a major depressive illness, specialized medical intervention may be required, i.e., anti-depressant medication.

Related to depressive features we should note that many mourners do have *transient* thoughts of suicide. Often the hope is of being reunited with the person who has died or thoughts may be present that this will allow him or her to escape the pain of the grief. While *transient* suicidal thoughts are normal and common, suicidal thoughts should always be assessed with utmost care.

Feelings of deprivation and impoverishment also are common during mourning. The person might long to be held, comforted, and simply wish to have that person who has died to talk to. The thought often is that the one person who understood him or her is gone and the mourner might feel abandoned by the person. Well known author C.S. Lewis[9] expressed his sense of deprivation following the death of his wife when he wrote: "Thought after thought, feeling after feeling, action after action had Helen for their target. Now their target is gone. I keep on, through habit, fitting an arrow to the string, then I remember that I have to lay the bow down."

The person who is not in an environment conducive to acknowledging and exploring experiences of intense loss, emptiness, and sadness will sometimes be in the position of being in conflict about expressing these feelings. Suppressed feelings often push for release, while the person is either discouraged by others, oneself, or both to repress them. The frequent result is an increased sense of isolation, loss, and sadness.

Clergyperson's Helping Role. The frequent and regular presence of a stabilizing person is critical during this time. Because this dimension of grief is so isolating, the opportunity to communicate one's feelings to an accepting and understanding person is one means of reconnecting with the world outside of oneself. One goal of helping is to keep the person from feeling totally isolated and abandoned during this difficult time. Many people respond to an outreach approach, as the sense of isolation may prevent them from directly asking for support and guidance.

As a helper you need to be sensitive to indirect cues and signals that relate to this dimension of grief. The majority of grieving persons do not directly bring up their need to talk about feelings of loss, emptiness, and sadness. However, indirect cues are given and when they go unheard, are misunderstood, or their urgency missed, the result is often another experience of loss for the person.

To counteract society's tendency to discourage the expression of these feelings, the griever needs to be encouraged to share thoughts and express tears. Feelings of loss, emptiness, sadness, even depression in the face of the death of loved ones, does not mean incompetence or that they should be ashamed of their feelings.

Avoid pushing for disclosure of painful feelings of loss until the person gives you cues of being at a point where those feelings can be shared with you. The person must feel a sense of respect from you as a helper prior to exploring painful feelings with you. The capacity to empathize with the depth of loss and sadness a person feels is often communicated through your nonverbal presence and when well established, the person will more openly begin to share innermost thoughts and feelings with you.

Another means of helping is to assist people in understanding the value in the temporary feelings of depression that come with grief. In a sense, this depression is nature's way of allowing for a time-out while one works to heal the wounds of grief. Depression slows down the physiological system and prevents major organ systems from being damaged.

Loss, emptiness, and sadness are part of acknowledging the reality of one's loss and experiencing them allows valuable time to begin re-ordering one's life. Depression that comes with grief can ultimately be used to move ahead, to assess old ways of being, and to make plans for the future. Only in allowing depression to slow oneself down do these opportunities present themselves. This process of reframing the person's depression as a positive part of the grief allows them to better tolerate these natural feelings in oneself.

RELIEF/RELEASE

Death can bring relief and release from suffering, particularly when the illness has been long and debilitating. Many people inhibit this normal dimension of their grief, fearing that others will think they are wrong or cruel to feel this way. So, while very natural, feelings of relief and release are often difficult for the griever to talk about and admit openly.

Relief does not equal a lack of feeling for the person who died, but instead relates to the griever's response to an end to painful suffering. In addition, to feel relief is natural because death frees one of certain demands and opens up new opportunities and experiences.

I recently saw a 40 year-old man in counseling following the death of his 38 year-old wife. His wife had been suffering with bone cancer for the past two years. Upon her death, he was able to acknowledge his relief that she was finally free of her pain. However, he also was able, with time, to acknowledge that the marital relationship of sixteen years had always been conflicted and unsatisfactory to him. He expressed release from their constant fights and his perception of their mutual chronic unhappiness in the relationship.

Feelings of relief and release also relate to the reality that we do not just begin to grieve at the moment of someone's death. The experience of grief begins when the person with whom we have a relationship enters the transition from being alive and living to dying.

When the dying process is prolonged and filled with physical and emotional pain for those involved, one might observe that family members experience some of the following thoughts over time: Initially a sense of "he is sick" toward "he is very sick" toward "he may die" toward "he is going to die" toward "he is suffering so much" toward "I'll be glad when he is out of his pain" toward "he is dead" toward, among a number of other thoughts and feelings "I'm relieved he is dead and out of his pain."

This process of changing thought patterns and experiences over time relates to the concept of *anticipatory grief*, a term first used by Erich Lindemann. Anticipatory grief is when emotional responses occur before an expected loss. To explore this concept in-depth would be to go beyond the primary purpose of this text. However, the reader is urged to familiarize himself or herself with this concept in the grief literature (See Question and Response on Anticipatory Grief on pages 131-133).

Death also can be experienced as relief when the apparent alternative is a continual debilitating journey with an unconscious vegetative form of existence, chronic alcoholism, and other forms of living that involves lack of quality. Regardless of how loving and caring a family may be, at times chronic illness exhausts and drains everyone. When death finally comes, relief is experienced not in isolation, but amongst a number of other emotions as well.

Another aspect of relief for some people is a sense of having been spared because someone else, not themselves died. Again, this sense of relief is natural and some persons will express a need to explore these feelings with you.

Crying and expressing the thoughts and feelings related to a loss also can be experienced as relief. I often witness a tremendous sense of relief from persons who have repressed and avoided the outward expression of their grief. Being able to acknowledge the pain of their experience frequently relieves internal pressure and allows them to make movement in the journey through their grief. To the mourner a sense of relief can occur by finding someone who is able to communicate an empathetic understanding of one's experience.

The relief that comes from acknowledging the pain of grief becomes a critical step toward reconciliation. As the pain is explored, acknowledged, and accepted as a vital part of healing, a renewed sense of meaning and purpose follows. Working to embrace relief as one of many normal feelings creates the opportunity to find hope beyond one's acute grief.

Clergyperson's Helping Role. The primary role of the helper is to allow for the expression of relief and communicate an understanding of it's naturalness. Listen acceptingly to the grievers sense of relief without implying or increasing any feelings of shame or guilt.

As previously noted, many people do feel guilty about the expression of a sense of relief. To many people it seems ungrateful and selfish. Work to help the person understand that relief certainly does not imply a lack of feeling for the person who died. The mourner's willingness to share components of the relief with you, speaks of the trust in you. Through the process of entering into a supportive dialogue with the griever you become a catalyst for the restoration of meaning and purpose in the person's life.

RECONCILIATION

The final dimension of grief in a number of proposed models is often referred to as resolution, recovery, reestablishment, or reorganization. This dimension often suggests a total return to "normalcy" and yet in my personal, as well as, professional experience—everyone is changed by the experience of grief. For the mourner to assume that life will be exactly as it was prior to the death is unrealistic and potentially damaging. Recovery as understood by some persons, mourners and caregivers alike, is all too often seen erroneously as an absolute, a perfect state of reestablishment.

Reconciliation is a term I believe to be more expressive of what occurs as the person works to integrate the new reality of moving forward in life without the physical presence of the person who has died. What occurs is a renewed sense of energy and confidence, an ability to fully acknowledge the reality of the death, and the capacity to become reinvolved with the activities of living. Also an acknowledgement occurs that pain and grief are difficult, yet necessary parts of life and living. (For a more extensive description of criteria for reconciliation, see Figure 7, page 63.)

As the experience of reconciliation unfolds the mourner recognizes that life will be different without the presence of the significant person who has died. A realization occurs that reconciliation is a process, not an event. Tasks involved in working through the completion of the emotional relationship with the person who has died, and re-directing of energy and initiative toward the future, often takes longer and involves more labor than most people are aware. We, as human beings, never "get over" our grief, but instead become reconciled to it.

We have noted that *the course of mourning cannot be prescribed* because it depends on many factors, such as, the nature of the relationship with the person who died, the availability and helpfulness of a support system, the nature of the death, and the ritual or funeral experience. As a result, despite how much we now know about dimensions of the grief experience, they will take different forms with different people. One of the major factors influencing the mourner's movement toward reconciliation is that he or she be allowed to mourn in his or her own unique way and time.

Reconciliation is the dimension wherein the full reality of the death becomes a part of the mourner. Beyond an intellectual working through is an emotional working through. What has been understood at the "head" level is now understood at the "heart" level—the person who was loved is dead. When a reminder such as holidays, anniversaries, or other special memories are triggered, the mourner experiences the intense pain inherent in grief, yet the duration and intensity of the pain is typically less severe as the healing of reconciliation occurs.

The pain changes from being ever-present, sharp, and stinging to an acknowledged feeling of loss that has given rise to renewed meaning and purpose. The sense of loss does not completely disappear yet softens and the intense pangs of grief become less frequent. Hope for a continued life emerges as the griever is able to make commitments to the future, realizing that the dead person will never be forgotten, yet knowing that one's own life can and will move forward.

In Figure 7 are criteria for reconciliation which are intended to give the reader some guidelines suggesting that the mourner has participated in the work of grief and emerged a whole and healthy person.

Clergyperson's Helping Role. Movement toward reconciliation is draining and exhausting, not only for the mourner but also for the helper who accompanies the person on the journey. In a general sense, being supportively present and helping the mourner "stay on track" are major helping tasks of the clergyperson. Grief is often so painful that people will attempt to avoid it at all costs (See Grief Avoidance Response Styles, pages 115-120). While avoidance may bring temporary relief, the work of grief is ultimately something that cannot be postponed.

Establishing the hope of reconciliation is central to the ultimate achievement of reconciliation. The majority of mourners experience a loss of confidence and esteem that leaves them questioning their capacity to heal. Those helpers that are able to supportively embrace a willingness to hope and expect reconciliation assist persons in movement toward their grief instead of away from it. This does not mean to deny pain, but a desire to "be with" persons in their pain and helplessness, all the while knowing that all wounds get worse before they get better.

Just as we expect that mourners experience pain as a part of reconciliation, when we expect reconciliation, and know it is possible, we help the person acknowledge reconciliation as a goal for which to work. However, if we as helpers somehow collaborate with those mourners who perceive that they will never move beyond the acute pain of their grief, we may well become a hindrance to their eventual healing.

Reconciliation from grief is normal. Yet, people need support, guidance, patience, perseverance, determination, and perhaps most of all hope and the belief in their capacity to heal. Part of the helping role is to serve as a catalyst that creates *conditions outside the person and qualities within the person* that make healing possible.

R. Scott Sullender[10] has written about the importance of the clergyperson's attitude related to the healing environment:

Those persons who have worked with their grief to move toward the dimension of reconciliation should be able to demonstrate:

— A recognition of the reality and finality of the death of the person who has died.

— A return to stable eating and sleeping patterns that were present prior to the death.

— A renewed sense of energy and personal well-being.

— A subjective sense of release or relief from the person who has died (they have thoughts of the person, but are not preoccupied with these thoughts).

— The capacity to enjoy experiences in life that should normally be enjoyable.

— The establishment of new and healthy relationships.

— The capacity to live a full life without feelings of guilt or lack of self-respect.

— The capacity to organize and plan one's life toward the future.

— The capacity to become comfortable with the way things are rather than attempting to make things as they were.

— The capacity to being open to more change in one's life.

— The awareness that one has allowed self to fully grieve and survived.

— The awareness that one does not "get over grief", but instead is able to acknowledge, "This is my new reality and I am ultimately the one who must work to create new meaning and purpose in my life."

— The capacity to acknowledge new parts of one's self that have been discovered in the growth through one's grief.

— The capacity to adjust to the new role changes that have resulted from the loss of the relationship.

— The capacity to be compassionate with oneself when normal resurgences of intense grief occur (holiday, anniversaries, special occasions).

— The capacity to acknowledge that the pain of loss is an inherent part of life that results from the ability to give and receive love.

Figure 7. Criteria for reconciliation.

NOTE: These criteria are intended to help you assess the mourner's movement toward reconciliation. Not every person will illustrate each of these criteria; however, the majority of the criteria should be present for the person to be considered beyond ENCOUNTER with the new reality. Many bereaved persons will attempt to convince themselves and others that they are further along in the healing process than they really are. Awareness of these criteria can help both them and you more appropriately assess their progress toward reconciliation.

The key criterion for a healing environment is attitude—an attitude of acceptance and openness to human feelings and human pain. People who are comfortable with their feelings are natural grievers and natural grief facilitators. People who are uncomfortable with their own feelings will grieve only with great anguish, pain and resistance. If we are to be effective pastoral care givers and agents of God's healing, we must be people who are comfortable with all sorts of human emotions. To be so comfortable with our own emotions, we must acknowledge, accept and freely share our own sorrow. (pp. 62)

So, just as the mourner's attitude toward the experience of grief influences the reconciliation process, the helper's attitude toward the healing environment invariably has a dramatic influence on bereavement outcome. To help people move toward reconciliation means to be open to your own experiences with grief while keeping the focus on those you are attempting to help. Obviously, if working on your grief ever becomes more important than working on their grief, you render yourself impotent as a helper.

As you work to support the reconciliation process you do not impose your own direction on the content of what is explored, rather, you allow the direction of the other's growth to guide what you do, to help determine how you respond in supportive, life-enhancing ways. You appreciate the person as being independent from you and respect his or her right to determine the direction of the growth. From a therapeutic stance, we can say that "we follow the lead that is provided us." (See pages 159-163 for further discussion of qualities of an effective helper during times of grief).

The process of helping another restore and renew self calls upon all of your personal strengths as a helper. While working with people involved in the pain of grief is often difficult, slow, and wearing, the work also can be enriching and fulfilling.

One last point regarding the process of reconciliation-for those persons wherein religious beliefs are important, it can be used as a support in their search for meaning and renewal. However, helpers from all backgrounds must be able to set aside their own religious beliefs or lack of them and make use of the framework of beliefs of the bereaved persons themselves.

I believe to help people find meaning in life following loss and transition is a true honor. Reconciliation is essential if the mourner is to once again live a satisfying, enriched life. Only through the renewal of purpose and meaning can grief become an influence for growth in the life of the mourner.

REFERENCES

[1] Bowlby, J. (1973). *Attachment and loss: Separation.* New York: Basic Books.

[2] Engel, G.L. (1971). Sudden and rapid death during psychological stress. *Annals of Internal Medicine, 74,* 771-782.

[3] Kübler-Ross, E. (1969). On Death and Dying. New York: Macmillan.

[4] Lindemann, E. (1944). Symptomatology and management of acute grief. *American Journal of Psychiatry, 101,* 141-148.

[5] Parkes, C.M. (1972). *Bereavement: Studies of grief in life.* New York: International Universities Press.

[6] Worden, J.W. (1982). *Grief counseling and grief therapy.* New York: Springer.

[7] Bowlby J. (1961). Processes of mourning. *International Journal of Psychoanalysis, 42,* 317-340.

[8] Glick, I.O., Weiss, R.S., & Parkey, C.M. (1974). *The first year of bereavement.* New York: John Wiley and Sons.

[9] Lewis, C.S. (1961). *A grief observed.* Greenwich, CT: Seabury Press.

[10] Sullender, R.S. (1985). *Grief and growth: Pastoral resources for emotional and spiritual growth.* New York: Paulist Press.

NOTES

8

ADDITIONAL SIGNIFICANT FEATURES OF GRIEF

You have provided a comprehensive overview of the experience of grief. Can you think of any other features of grief that are appropriate to emphasize?

While I have attempted to provide an overview of the experience of grief I do think helpful procedure would be to briefly review some additional features that the helper may well encounter.

TIME DISTORTION

The mourner often experiences a distorted sense of time. On occasion, time may seem to move quickly while at other times it moves slowly. The person's sense of past and future may seem frozen in place. Many mourners will lose track of the time of day or the day of the week. This normal experience of time distortion is sometimes a major contributor to the "going crazy syndrome".

An excellent illustration of time distortion is provided in the reflective thought of Diane Kennedy Pike as quoted in the book *The Courage To Grieve*[1]:

> I needed to set my own pace for the journey. It might have seemed to someone looking on from the outside that I was walking in place, or even dragging my feet, for I was not ready to turn my attention to the future for many months. But from inside the experience, I was moving as quickly as I could, covering enormous segments of land with a rapidity that used all my energy. Only I could know how much time I needed to make each leg of the journey. (p. 84)

This woman's experience speaks to how the helper must respect how time distortion creates confusion about the past, present, and future. Helping the mourner create a balance between remembering the past, acknowledging the present, and hoping for the future is an appropriate therapeutic stance to adopt. Allowing and encouraging memories of the past assists in freeing the mourner from the emotional investment of the past; therefore, making possible, a hopeful feeling about the present and future

OBSESSIONAL REVIEW OR RUMINATION

Obsessional review or ruminating is another normal part of the healing process. This is where events and memories of the person are reviewed and relived over and over again in one's mind. This review serves a vital need to integrate the emotional and cognitive realities of the death. Many mourners express a wish that they could block this phenomenon out only to discover that this is impossible.

If the mourner is unaware of the healing qualities inherent in this process of review, they may punish themselves for the inability to discontinue ruminating. Yet, the review process must be done repeatedly over time to break the emotional bonds that link them to the deceased. Helping mourners and those around them be tolerant of the time and work involved in this process is painful, but as with all wounds the course is one of getting worse before getting better.

SEARCH FOR MEANING

Closely related to the process of obsessional review is the phenomenon of the search for meaning. This can be described as an attempt to make sense out of what has happened. The bereaved works to put the death in a perspective that he or she can understand. With a number of variations, examples including, "Why him?", "Why this way?", "Why Now?"—the mourner longs to find some meaning in an event that is threatening to the past and present and assaults the sense of the future. This search for meaning often occurs in the context of the obsessional review process previously outlined.

While the mourner seldom anticipates finding "the answer" to the many questions, the searching occurs in part secondary to efforts to tolerate the loss. As the wrestling with "why?" questions evolves, the majority of persons can compile a list of a hundred reasons why the deceased should not have died under these circumstances or at this time. The existential issue is one of how the mourner confronts the suffering at this time. Asking questions in the search for meaning, is, once again, a normal part of this process.

As the person searches for meaning the helper must be careful to be supportively responsive without attempting to offer answers. Mourners typically do not find comfort in pat responses to questions they know are not easy to answer. The healing occurs in the opportunity to pose the questions as opposed to answering them. Supportive companionship and responsive listening are the primary helping orientations that allow the person to come to an understanding while exploring religious values, questioning the philosophy of life, and renewing the resources for living.

As clergy know from experience, grief often results in the mourner asking "why" questions in relationship to God as he or she searches for meaning in the death. The mourner's former beliefs about God are often questioned and explored when opportunity is provided to do so. Of course, not judging persons' need to question, but instead "being with" them and supporting their need to question is inherently helpful to the healing process. Many mourners have taught me that in being allowed and encouraged to question God, they ultimately discover a new, more mature relationship with God. They often express an image of God that is not all powerful and is not making decisions about who, how, and when people will die, but rather an image of God that is also saddened by their loss and is comforting to them even in the depth of their sorrow. However, this understanding only occurs over time as opportunities to re-work their relationship with God are provided.

IS THIS DEATH GOD'S WILL?

For those persons where religion is a part of their life often the question is asked, "Is this death God's will? This questioning frequently occurs as a part of the previously described phenomenon of the search for meaning.

For the person who holds a perception of an all powerful God this question can be particularly difficult. They might reason, "If God loves me how can He take this most precious person from me?" Of course, this same person may have been told by family and friends, "It is God's will and you should just accept it and go on." However, the subjective experience of the mourner is often that God is punishing the person for some misdeed or indiscretion or that, "If this is the will of God, what right do I have to grieve?" Consequently, the person may develop a pattern of denying and repressing the grief. Attempts to comfort with "It is God's will" serves to minimize, if not totally ignore, the possible feelings of the mourner. Again the more helpful orientation to assisting is to be willing to "be with" the person and responsively listen as they communicate the need to explore this question of God's will. The evolution of a level of understanding that perceives God as suffering with the mourner appears to have meaning for a number of people. Two resources that some people find helpful in this sensitive area are the books by Kushner, *When Bad Things Happen to Good People*[2], and by Weatherhead, *The Will of God*.[3]

TRANSITIONAL OBJECTS

Transitional objects are belongings of the person who has died that take on special meaning. The more familiar term for some is *security blanket*. These objects serve as symbolic means of fusion to the person who has died and is normal behavior.

The mourner finds that having objects such as clothing provide a sense of feeling close to the deceased person. For example, one recently bereaved widow found herself sleeping with one of her dead husbands favorite shirts "As I clutched his shirt close to me, I didn't feel so alone. As I worked with my grief, my need for the shirt dwindled over time."

Mourners often will ask people around them if they should do away with familiar objects that belonged to the deceased. This is a question typically more effectively answered in a reflective way based on the needs of the individual person. To do away with familiar objects too soon frequently takes away some of the sense of security these very objects provide. Once the person has moved toward reconciliation, he or she is usually in a better position to decide what to do with belongings. Simply doing away with objects of the person who has died does not equate with emotional healing. Unfortunately, sometimes the mourner, friends, family, and caregivers think this in the case and prematurely take away some of this valuable sense of security.

SUICIDAL THOUGHTS

While previously described under the dimension of grief titled, *loss/emptiness/sadness,* suicidal thoughts are important enough to re-emphasize. Transient thoughts of suicide appear to be a normal and common part of the experience of grief. However, if these thoughts of self-destruction persist over time or take on planning and structure, the need for professional intervention becomes paramount. Suicidal thoughts can sometimes be an expression of wanting to find relief from the pain of grief, or be experienced as a desire to reunite with the person who has died. All helpers to the bereaved would be well served to obtain special training in assessing the risk of suicide.

SUDDEN CHANGES IN MOOD

Another expected observation of the helper is the dramatic mood changes you may see in the mourner. The person may be feeling better one minute and in the depths of sadness the next. Often confusion surrounds this experience because many mourners expect that they should follow a pattern of continually feeling better. Sudden mood changes can be triggered by such things as a fleeting thought of the deceased, an insensitive comment from a friend, or changes in the weather. As the movement toward reconciliation occurs, the frequency of mood changes usually lessen and the periods of hopelessness are replaced by periods of hopefulness. However, again, this only occurs in the presence of an understanding support system.

SUBJECTIVE NATURE OF GRIEF

The experience of grief, by its very nature creates a turning inward on the part of the mourner. This temporary self-focus is necessary for psychological survival. Turning inward toward self is a form of protection against outside forces that threaten the mourner's desire to hold on to the internalized image of the person who has died. Mourners often fear that persons around them will attempt to force them to give up this need to hang on before they are ready to let go. Unfortunately, as we discussed under the social influences of grief their experience sometimes bears this out. Some persons will attempt to "take grief away from them" and attempt to force a re-entry into the world before the mourner has had the opportunity to temporarily retreat as a form of survival. Understanding and allowing for this normal self-orientation is essential to the helping role.

Obviously, if the self-focus becomes prolonged the person may be protecting self from sharing the grief outside of oneself; therefore, stunting the movement through the experience of grief. Movement beyond this self-focus is more likely to occur when it is understood and allowed for as opposed to being forced onto the mourner. The long-standing nature of the person's personality also will influence the need for alone time and inward focus.

Some helpers become threatened by the mourner's self focus and perceive it as a rejection of the helping efforts. Again, becoming comfortable with this temporary withdrawal is essential to the helper's ultimate capacity to be supportive and assist in the healing process. This process is analogous to what occurs when we have a physical wound. We often cover it with a bandage for a period of time before exposing it to the open air and all of its healing properties as well as contaminants. The emotional pain of grief certainly demands the same kind of respect.

REFERENCES

[1]   Tatelbaum, J. (1980). *The courage to grieve.* New York: Harper and Row.

[2]   Kushner, H.S. (1981). *When bad things happen to good people.* New York: Avon Books.

[3]   Weatherhead, L.D. (1944). *The will of God.* Nashville: Abington Press.

9

RECONCILIATION NEEDS OR TASKS OF MOURNING

Do bereaved people have some tasks they need to do to be able to reach the dimension you refer to as reconciliation?

A helpful concept for both the mourner and the caregiver is that of "tasks" of mourning. The mourner's awareness of these tasks of grief work can help give a participative, action-oriented outlook of the experience of grief as opposed to a perception of grief as being a phenomenon that is simply experienced in a passive manner. For the caregiver a knowledge of these tasks of mourning provides a framework for outlining a significant portion of one's helping role.

A series of tasks must be achieved if the mourner is to reach toward reconciliation. The caregiver directs his or her efforts toward these tasks. Several researchers have described their perceptions of these tasks. Erich Lindermann[1] a pioneer in grief investigation described primarily three tasks that he believed to be necessary to the work of grief:

1. emancipation from the bondage of the deceased,

2. readjustment to the environment in which the deceased is missing, and

3. formation of new relationships.

Worden[2] outlined what he described as four tasks of mourning:

1. to accept the reality of the loss,

2. to experience the pain of the grief,

3. to adjust to an environment in which the deceased is missing, and

4. to withdraw emotional energy and reinvest it in another relationship.

Parkes and Weiss[3] have identified three tasks that must occur for healing to take place:

1. intellectual recognition and explanation of the loss,

2. emotional acceptance of the loss, and

3. assumption of a new identity.

Obviously, overlap is present in these different investigators' perceptions of the tasks of mourning. What follows is this author's perception of what could be termed. *Reconciliation Needs* or *Tasks of Mourning.* Again, you will note similarity with other investigators in perception of the mourner's needs. Following each task are questions for you, as a helper, to ask yourself as you assess the mourner's progress toward reconciliation.

Five Reconciliation Needs of the Mourner and the Caregiver's Helping Role

1. To experience and express outside of oneself the reality of the death.

This reconciliation need involves confronting the reality that the person loved has died and will not return. Such acknowledgment only comes after opportunities are provided to talk about the nature of the death and repetitious confrontation with thoughts, feelings, and memories of the person who has died. Typically, this full sense of reality does not come until several months after the death. Prior to this time the mourner works to distance self from the pain that comes from acknowledging the reality. When acknowledgement of reality does occur, intellectual realization precedes emotional realization. However, both levels of realization must occur for this task to be accomplished.

Questions To Ask Self As Helper

Where is the person in terms of confronting the reality that their loved one has died?

Is time a factor in where the person is in relation to accomplishing this task?

Do I need to respect the person's need to push away some of the full sense of reality for a period of time while attempting to help the person gently confront this new reality?

Is the person using unhealthy protective mechanisms, such as alcohol abuse, overeating, or impulsive spending of money as means of avoiding this task?

What can I as a helper do or be for this person that will help the work on this task?

2. To tolerate the emotional suffering that is inherent in the work of grief while nurturing oneself both physically and emotionally.

This task involves the expression of a wide range of thoughts and feelings that result from the death of the loved person. In addition, this task incorporates the need to care for oneself from both a physical and emotional perspective.

The thoughts and feelings experienced result from the *encounter* with new reality of the death; the confusion, the helplessness, the fear,—essentially the pain of the grief and the resulting emotional suffering must be absorbed. If avoided, denied, or repressed, the movement toward reconciliation is inhibited. This task is often more difficult for males than females because of social conditioning related to lack of emotional expression.

Another form of keeping oneself from working on this task is to idealize or glorify the person who had died. Through the process of glorification the mourner may demonstrate an unwillingness to confront any painful thoughts and feelings related to the loss. While really no way exists to avoid this task if reconciliation is to be reached, some people become experts at postponing the inevitable.

The other component of this reconciliation need is the need to care for and nurture oneself both physically and emotionally while experiencing the emotional suffering described above. While this seems fairly self-evident many mourners need practical assistance in seeing that these needs are not neglected. Davidson[4] has provided an excellent framework for the mourner's, self-care related to emotional and physical well-being. He stated that present research suggests five factors have been found useful in identifying those mourners who are likely to adapt healthily. These factors, and a brief description of each are as follows:

a. A Nurturing, Supportive Social Network

As emphasized as a theme throughout this book a supportive social support system is vital to the healing process. During a time of disorientation, understanding support allows for the beginning of reorientation. Human contact is essential to emotional and physical well being.

b. Adequate Nutritional Balance

Davidson pointed out that no matter how different people are in age, race, size, appearance, activity, or religion, each person needs the same nutrients: protein, fat, carbohydrates,, vitamins, minerals, and water. Mourners need daily portions of food from each of the four basic food groups:

- Milk—yogurt, cheese, ice cream, cottage cheese
- Meat—lean red meat, poultry, or fish
- Fruit and vegetables—as fresh and unprocessed as possible
- Grains—whole grains or fortified or enriched grain products

c. Adequate Fluid Intake

Adequate fluids are needed to carry away the body's toxic waste and maintain appropriate electrolyte balance. Because mourners have a tendency to override their sense of thirst, they need to drink more fluids than they think they need. Beverages with caffeine (coffee, colas, many pre-mixed beverages), which tend to cause further dehydration, should be avoided. Alcohol also should be avoided.

d. Daily Exercise

Davidson emphasized the importance of daily full range-of-motion exercise. Walking vigorously for more than 20 minutes at a time each day, various stretching regimens, and aerobic activities are examples of appropriate exercise. He also pointed out the positive role of exercise in the control of depression.

e. Daily Rest

Among suggestions here are that regular rituals for rest need to come at the same time in each 24-hour cycle even if sleeping is impossible. While sleeping in a pattern to which one is normally accustomed may be difficult, maintaining a regular routine of rest, even during the day, will prove helpful.

Questions To Ask Self As Helper

Has the person allowed self to experience the pain of the grief?

If so, with whom has he or she shared the grief?

Was the person provided with a sense of feeling understood in the expression of the grief?

Is the person caring for self physically and emotionally during this vulnerable time?

How is the person functioning in relation to the five factors for healthy mourning previously outlined?

What can I as a helper do or be for this person that will help the work on this task?

3. To convert the relationship with deceased from one of presence to a relationship of memory.

This reconciliation need requires what Freud[5] described as "decathexis". This is where the mourner works to modify and detach the emotional ties to the person who has died in preparation to live in an altered relationship with the dead person. The working to convert the nature of the relationship is what Irion[6] described as "movement along a continuum from a relationship of presence (i.e., living, interactive, responsive relationship) to a relationship of memory."

Emotionally the mourner should not be expected to give up all ties and bonds that have been a part of his or her life with the person who died. To communicate to the mourner that any and all relationships with the deceased are over is unwise. However, an alteration must occur of the relationship from one of presence to one of memory. Memories that are precious, occasional dreams reflecting the significance of the relationship, and living legacies are among the influences that give testimony to a different form of a continued relationship.

Instead, a healthy reconciliation to the death requires the achievement of a new form of relationship firmly rooted in the context of memory. Accomplishing the evolution of this type of relationship often provides a sense of meaning to the mourner. As a helper you have the privilege of assisting in the achievement of this task.

Questions To Ask Self As Helper

Where is the person in the process of converting the relationship from one of presence to one of memory?

Is the person resisting any alteration in the nature of viewing the relationship as one of presence?

If so, what contributing factors may be influencing this stance (i.e., nature of the relationship with the deceased, long-standing personality of the mourner)?

Is the person's perception that he or she must give up all forms of bonding to the deceased?

What can I do to help embrace natural forms of a new type of relationship rooted in memory (i.e., stimulation of memories, the expression of dreams, the sharing of living legacies)?

What can I as a helper do or be for this person that will help the work on this task?

4. To develop a new self-identity based on a life without the deceased.

This reconciliation need relates to the evolution of a new self-identity that reflects the reality of the loss and its consequences. The development of a new identity occurs over an extended period of time as the work of mourning progresses. A redefined identity involves many aspects of one's being: role confusion as the person struggles to move from being a "we" to an "I"; struggles with a changed social status; the questioning of one's self-worth; doubts about the future; and fears related to a new found autonomy.

Clinical experience suggests that women find that working on this reconciliation need is more difficult than it is for men. Historically, a woman's self-identity is more tied to role as a wife or mother. However, women are more likely than men to seek out support and guidance as they struggle with the development of this new self-identity.

Questions To Ask Self As Helper

Where is this person in the process of forming a new self-identity?

Is time a factor in influencing where the person is in working on this reconciliation need?

What are the role changes that this person is experiencing as a result of the death?

Are role models of persons who have gone through similar experiences available to them?

What can I as a helper do or be for this person that will help the work on this task?

5. To relate the experience of loss to a context of meaning.

This reconciliation need relates to renewing one's resources for living and discovering some sense of meaning in the death. In the process of working on this task the mourner will typically question his or her philosophy of life and explore religious values.

This task is intertwined with the "search for meaning" as described on pages 68-69.

When someone loved dies the mourner's perception of meaning and purpose in life is changed and sometimes severely complicated and conflicted. Even for those persons for whom faith in God has been an important part of their life, to seek a new understanding of God in the context of this deep sense of loss is still natural. A newly formed set of beliefs typically only evolves after a prolonged period of confusion and questioning. The helper's knowledge of this reconciliation need and capacity to "be with" the person is essential as the mourner works to discover a context of meaning in the experience.

Questions To Ask Self As Helper

Where is the person in the process of relating the experience of loss to a context of meaning?

What were the persons religious and philosophical beliefs about life prior to the loss?

How has the loss altered these beliefs?

Does the person give self permission to question previously held beliefs?

Is the person punishing self for naturally questioning these beliefs?

What can I as a helper do or be for this person that will help the work on this task?

This outline of reconciliation needs is provided in an effort to assist the helper in having a sense of some of the many tasks that are placed before the mourner. The content is not intended to provide comprehensive coverage of all aspects of the counseling role. The responsibilities of the helper are complex and ever changing as the mourner proceeds to do the grief work necessary for healing to occur. Each of these outlined reconciliation needs is accompanied by its own challenges and stresses to both the mourner and the helper. To be of assistance, you as a caregiver must (1) allow yourself to emphatically enter into the pain of the mourner, (2) work to understand the challenges being presented to the mourner, and (3) develop a wide range of helpful skills that assists the person in reconciling the loss.

REFERENCES

[1] Lindemann, E. (1944). Symptomatology and management of acute grief, *American Journal of Psychiatry*, Pages 101, 141-148.

[2] Worden, J.W. (1982). *Grief counseling and grief therapy*. New York: Springer.

[3] Parkes, L.M. & Weiss, R.S. (1983). *Recovery from bereavement*. New York: Basic Books.

[4] Davidson, G.W. (1984). *Understanding mourning: A guide for those who grieve*. Minneapolis: Augusburg Publishing House.

[5] Freud, S. (1957). Mourning and melancholia. In *Standard edition of complete psychological works of Sigmund Freud, (Vol.14)*. London: Hogarth Press.

[6] Irion, P. (1976). The funeral and the bereaved. In Pine V.R., et al. (Eds), *Acute grief and the funeral*. Publishers. Springfield, IL: Charles C. Thomas.

NOTES

10
MORBIDITY AND
MORTALITY

Are any research studies available that provide us with information on bereavement as it relates to morbidity and mortality?

The growing body of knowledge related to grief now consists of a number of studies that illustrate bereavement leaves the survivors at higher risk for both morbidity and mortality. Increased vulnerability to illness and death is an area that demands further research; however, evidence to date appears to support a correlation between bereavement and mortality and morbidity. What follows is a brief overview of the findings from several studies. For the reader interested in more detailed information he or she is referred to the references at the conclusion of this section.

Dating back to 1944, Lindemann[1] reported that mourners experience high risk levels for seven deadly diseases: Heart attack, cancers of the gastrointestinal track, high blood pressure, nuerodermatitis, rheumotoid arthritis, diabetes, and thyroid malfunction. Rees and Lutkins[2] 1967 studies supported Lindemann's findings.

In 1977, Rowland[3] reported the results of a comprehensive review of numerous investigations documenting significant increases in illness and in death for mourners, particularly during the first six months after the death. According to Rees and Lutkins[4] this appears to be true not only for widows, but for parents, as well as siblings. In looking specifically at cardiac patients, Lynch[5], also in 1977, reported that mourners experience two to two-and-one-half times the normal risk for heart attack when compared to non-mourners, and dependent on the region where they live, three to three-and-one-half times the risk for cancers of gastrointestinal tract.

Additional studies[6,7,8] suggest increased risk of drug abuse, alcohol dependence, nueroendocrine disorders, electrolyte disorders, and suppressed immune function. Apparently some of the changes in the bodies functioning may be influenced by abnormal production of steriods, particularly cortisol.[9,10]

A study in England in 1963 of 4500 widowers over the age of 54 found a major increase (almost 40%) in their death rate during the first six months after bereavement, after which it dropped back to expected levels.[11] Upon further analysis of this same study in 1969, a very high portion of the causes of death was found to be due to heart disease.[12] In a 1970 study of widows in London by Parkes[13] that focused on the first year of bereavement the finding was that regardless of age, women whose spouses have died are more likely to die themselves or to be emotionally or physically ill than are married women.

Two separate reviews of the literature, one in 1977[14], the other in 1983[15] reported that when compared with marriage, widowhood was related to high mortality for both sexes, with excess risk being greater for men and the younger widowed. The 1983 study found that the highest risk for mortality for widows appeared to be during the second year of bereavement; whereas, for widowers the risk for mortality was greatest during the first six months. So it seems that people may literally die of a "broken heart."

The significance of preventative intervention in bereavement care is highlighted by reviewing the studies identified in this section of the book. While we still have much to learn, enough evidence exists to suggest that bereavement is a time of increased risk in the areas of both morbidity and mortality. Just think— effective counsel at a time of grief may add years of living to another fellow human being's life.

REFERENCES

[1] Lindemann, E. (1944). Symptomatology and management of acute grief. *American Journal of Psychiatry*, 101:148.

[2] Rees, W.D., & Lutkins, S.G. (1967). The mortality of bereavement. *British Medical Journal*, 4:13-16.

3   Rowland, K.F. (1977). Environmental events predicting death for the elderly. *Psychological Bulletin, 84,* 349-372.

4   Rees, W.D., & Lutkins, S.G. (1967) The mortality of Bereavement. *British Medical Journal, 4:*13-16.

5   Lynch, J.J., (1977). *The broken heart: The medical consequences of loneliness.* New York: Basic Books.

6   Bartrop, R., et al. (1977). Depressed lymphocyte function after bereavement. *Lancet, 1,* 834-836.

7   Hofer, M.A., (1984). Relationships as regulators: A psychobiological perspective on bereavement. *Psychosomatic Medicine, 46,* 183-197.

8   Osterweis, M., Solomon, F., & Green, M. (eds). (1984). *Bereavements: Functions, Consequences, and Care.* Washington, D C: National Academy Press.

9   Hofer, M.A., Wolff, C.T., Friedman, S.B., & Mason, J.W. (1972). "Psychoendocrine study of bereavement: Part I: Hydroxycorticosteroid excretion rates of parents following death of their children from leukemia. *Psychosomatic Medicine, 34,* 481-491.

10   Hofer, M.A., Wolff, C.T., Friedman, S.B., & Mason, J.W. (1972). Psychoendocrine study of bereavement: Part II: Observations on the process of mourning in relation to adrenocortical function. *Psychosomatic Medicine, 34,* 492-504.

11   Young, M., Benjamin, B., & Wallis, C. (1963). Mortality of widowers. *Lancet, 2,* 454-546.

12   Parkes, C.M., Benjamin, B., & Fitzgerald, R.G. (1969). Broken heart: A statistical study of increased mortality among widowers. *British Medical Journal, 1,* 740-743.

13   Parkes, C.M. (1970). The first year of bereavement: A longitudnal study of the reaction of London widows to the death of their husbands. *Psychiatry, 33,* 444-467.

14   Jacobs, S., & Ostfeld, A. (1977). An epidemiological review of the mortality of bereavement. *Psychosomatic Medicine, 39,* 344-3557.

15   Stroebe, M.S., & Stroebe, W. (1983). Who suffers more? Sex differences in health risks of the widowed. *Psychological Bulletin, 93,* 179-301.

NOTES

11

COMPLICATED GRIEF

I have heard the term "pathological grief". What is it? Do different types exist and, if so, how would you define them?

A most difficult, yet important task for the helper is to be able to differentiate normal grief from so-called "pathological grief." The use of the terms "pathological" or "abnormal" are confusing terms. The reason for the confusion is that what is normal behavior in times of grief is often contrary to what is generally thought to be normal, healthy, adjustive behavior. So, what would normally seem pathological or abnormal is perfectly normal in grief.

Historically, attempts have been made to define those characteristics that are common to normal grief as opposed to characteristics that are common to pathological grief. We are now aware that this descriptive approach is insufficient as a means of differential classification. Distinguishing normal grief from pathological grief is primarily related to the intensity of a response or the duration of a response rather than to the presence or absence of a specific characteristic of mourning. So many individual differences and cultural variations exist in mourning process that to clearly define what is normal and what is not is all but impossible.

My personal bias is to suggest that the terms pathological, abnormal, unresolved, and atypical not be used at all. My rationale for the abolishment of these terms is that I frequently discover that caregivers are sometimes quick to use these terms out of a lack of understanding for the mourner's experience—the result being that distance is created in the helping relationship. The reasoning sometimes is as follows: "Well, the person is having a pathological response so there really isn't anything I can do for them." In other words, framing a mourner's response as abnormal or pathological appears to result in some helpers abandoning the very persons who are most in need of help.

The term I prefer to see used is "complicated grief." This may seem to be purely a semantic distinction. However, I have found that in making this distinction the helper is able to perceive that *just because the response is complicated does not mean that with appropriate counsel it cannot become uncomplicated.* A more hopeful, life-enhancing approach is taken when the helper has a belief that he or she has the knowledge and tools to uncomplicate the mourning process.

Multiple reasons exist for which a person's experience with grief might become complicated. Two primary reasons are outlined.

1. The social learning that occurs within one's family and/or culture.

As discussed earlier in this text, "being strong" in one's grief is often seen as being courageous. To deny and repress pain, to control tears, and to suffer in silence may be modeled as admirable behavior. However, when the mourner attempts to maintain these ideals, he or she typically denies the pain inherent in the experience and it becomes complicated.

2. Lack of knowledge, or inaccurate knowledge about experiencing and reconciling the mourning process.

Many people simply lack knowledge about the grief process itself. Few people will naturally experience grief smoothly and easily without first using more altered ways of coping with loss. This sets the mourner up for a complicated journey through grief from the very beginning. For those persons who have never had a previous experience with death, they have not had the opportunity to develop resources to cope.

The reader wanting more detailed information on the conditions that may predispose the mourner to complicated grief will find Lazare's[1] outline of both the psychological and social influences to be of help. Those factors that influence individual responses (see pages 25-32) also can impact on the potential of the complicated grief response.

Having acknowledged that no ideal system of classification for complicated grief has been given does not reduce the importance of attempting to develop some means of identifying when someone has strayed off course. A number of investigators have outlined their impressions of what is referred to in this text as complicated grief. What follows is a brief review of the existing literature. Differences of opinion on what constitutes disordered variants of grief reinforce the subjective nature of psychological diagnosis.

One of the first efforts to distinguish between normal and complicated mourning was Freud's[2] classic article on mourning and melancholia. His primary approach was descriptive in nature and subsequent studies have suggested that some of the character- istics Freud described as abnormal grief are actually observed in normal grief responses found in random populations. So while we might appreciate our friend Sigmund's efforts, our knowledge has advanced beyond this point.

Lindemann's[3] paradigm of abnormal grief focuses on distorted reactions and delayed reactions. He outlined the following criteria: overactivity without a sense of loss; the acquisition of symptoms of the last illness of the deceased, the development of recognized medical disease, alterations in relationships with friends and relatives, furious hostility toward specific persons such as doctors, schizophreniform behavior, lasting loss of patterns of social interaction, self-destructive behaviors, and agitated depressions. Again, we know that variants of some of these criteria can now be considered within the realm of normal grief.

Bowlby[4] acknowledged the difficulties inherent in the classi- fication process and was in agreement with Lindemann that the two main influences of pathological responses are best described as delayed reactions (prolonged absence of conscious grieving) and distorted responses (chronic mourning). Siggins[5] defined a morbid grief reaction as a noticeable exaggeration of any of the responses typical to the grief process.

Welu[6] provided the following criteria for what he termed pathological bereavement: self destructive behavior, suicidal thoughts or feelings, physiological problems, social withdrawal, depressive states with obvious clinical symptoms, hospitalization for psychiatric symptoms, and the taking of psychotherapuetic drugs. Once again, depending on the clinician with whom you talk, some of these criteria would be considered within the realm of normal grief. Obviously, differences of opinion would center on the matter of degree or exaggeration of these symptoms.

One other example that illustrates the subjective nature of some of the criteria that has evolved over this issue is provided by DeVaul and Zisook.[7] They outlined three guidelines for what they termed unresolved grief: Painful response when the deceased is mentioned, realization of grief by the individual, and unaccountable depression or the emergence of medical symptoms on the anniversary of the loss.

Since complicated grief is becoming more pervasive in our society, the need for more uniform ways of identifying the complicated grief experience becomes even more important. Once persons have been identified that need additional help we need to be willing to enter into the process of helping uncomplicate their experience.

CATAGORIES OF COMPLICATED GRIEF

The following classifications reflect a compilation of the most contemporary thinking about identifying complicated grief. These descriptions have been adapted from the work of several investigators [8-12] including my own clinical experience.

1. Absent Grief

In absent grief no apparent feelings of grief are expressed. The person may project a picture as if the death never occurred. While initial feelings of denial are a natural means of attempting to cope, prolonged denial indicates a complicated grief response that demands attention. Absent grief often appears to be influenced by what Lifton[13] has referred to as "psychic numbing"—the inability of the person to meaningfully incorporate the reality of the death into his or her symbolic framework. The incapacity to feel due to blocking can and does result in emotional and physical turmoil for the mourner.

2. Distorted Grief

In distorted grief a distortion occurs in one or more of the normal dimensions of grief. This distortion may prevent the grief process from unfolding and the person often becomes fixated on the distorted dimension of the grief. For example, the person may keep self so angry that other feelings (loss, sadness, hurt) are not acknowledged and explored. Clinical experiences suggest that anger and guilt are the two dimensions that most frequently become distorted. In working to understand causes of this distorted response one often discovers factors related to the existence of long-term ambivalent or dependent relationships.

3. Converted Grief

In converted grief the person demonstrates behaviors and symptoms which result in personal distress; however, he or she is unable to relate their presence to the loss. A classic example of this is the person who has multiple physical complaints with no organic findings (somatization disorder). These persons need to protect themselves from the pain of the grief is often unconscious, and, therefore results in this conversion response. I have outlined elsewhere in this text (see pages 115-120) typical forms of what I have termed "grief avoidance response styles."

4. Chronic Grief

In chronic grief the person demonstrates a persistent pattern of intense grief that does not result in appropriate reconciliation. The continued foci are on the person who has died, over valuing objects that belonged to the deceased, and depressive brooding. Essentially, the mourner attempts to keep the person alive. Unfortunately, some people believe that if they really loved the person who died they must prolong their intense grief.

People around the mourner sometimes enable, maintain, or reinforce this presentation of chronic grief out of a lack of knowledge of how to facilitate movement toward reconciliation. While the mourner will be forever changed by the loss, the evolution of a chronic mourning pattern will result in an inability to continue living until one dies.

How do you go about assessing if a person is experiencing a complicated grief response?

I find that some people will seek help for what they typically identify as "feeling stuck" or a recognition that grief is impacting on their lives in ways that prevent them from living as fully as they would like. The task of the helper at that point becomes one of being capable of assessing the potential complicators. In addition, in any initial assessment the potential of complicated grief should always be included.

Of course, knowledge of the four catagories of complicated grief previously outlined is essential. Beyond that I have made a practice of using Barton's[14] scheme for the assessment of complicated grief. As described below, his model is comprehensive and easily lends itself to an enhanced understanding of potential complicators. These criteria should only be considered a guide to help frame the helper's clinical knowledge.

1. Complicating Factors Related to the Death Itself

- Suddenness of death without adequate time for psychological preparation.

- Death considered exceptionally untimely, as in the death of a child or young adult.

- Mode of death considered incomprehensible, as in suicides.

- Ambiguity and unsureness about the death, with questioning of its actual occurrence, e.g., marked deterioration or mutilation of the dead person to the point that the feeling is that the person actually has not died.

- Absence or isolation from the occurrences surrounding the death resulting in inadequate sensory perceptions for the acknowledgment of its reality.

- A sense of having "participated" in the actual event causing the death accompanied by excessive guilt, e.g., the driver of an automobile involved in a wreck in which someone else is killed.

2. Complicating Factors Related to the Survivor's Psychological Traits

- Unresolved feelings and conflict related to earlier losses in the persons life.

- Tendencies toward depression or established difficulty in managing loss.

- Difficulties in expressing and managing feelings of sadness and anger.

- Extreme dependency on the reflected appraisals of others and the need for excessive approval by others, especially in the expression of feelings.

- A tendency toward assuming inappropriate levels of responsibility and the presence of excessive guilt over perceived failure related to the death.

- Excessive dependency on others to meet needs based on actual limited personal resources.

- A tendency to form markedly ambivalent relationships with others characterized by both loving and hating those persons.

- Survivor too young to conceptualize and integrate the finality of the loss.

- Limited options in terms of developing new life styles separate from those shared with the lost person.

- Failure to establish independent existence due to undermining of independence by others with whom the survivor relates—forced dependency.

3. Complicating Factors Related to the Survivor's Relationship With the Lost Person

- Extreme levels of identification with the lost person.

- The presence of intensely ambivalent feelings toward the deceased.

- Intensely close relationship with the lost person to the exclusion of any close relationship with others.

- Excessive and continued reliance on established life patterns with the pretense of a continued relationship with the dead person.

- The presence of unresolved conflict involving the lost person.

- Extreme dependency on the lost person for validation of self, identity, and meaning related activities—an inability to see oneself as a separate person.

- The deceased individual having been excessively dependent on the survivor.

- Excessive guilt related to the life events and death of the deceased accompanied by intense sense of personal responsibility.

- Excessive and prolonged survivor's guilt.

4. Complicating Factors Related to the Inability to Express Feelings Related to the Loss

- Inability of the survivor to be accepting of the high level of feelings surrounding the loss of the person. Suppression of the expression of feelings as an act of protectiveness toward others.

- Inability of other family members to legitimize the feelings related to grief.

- Failure of caregivers to legitimize the feelings surrounding the grief process.

- Other intense and extreme losses or compounded losses occurring at the same time.

- Interpersonal disruption in the individual's environment which disallows the grief process.

- Survivor unable to participate in the grief process during the established grief period due to his or her own physical incapacitation.

- Lack of access to usual rituals or belief systems employed in the management of loss and the grief process.

- Insistence by others that the survivors's grief be managed in a specific manner, i.e., intolerance.

- Dislocation of the person from the usual interpersonal context which is important and supportive in his or her expression of feelings.

- Dislocation from the usual sociocultural and religious context for the expression of grief.

- Excessive use of drugs or alcohol to suppress feelings connected with grief.

- Conversion of the expression of grief feelings to unrecognized symbolic expressions (as in identification symptoms involving physical symptoms).

- Extreme interpersonal isolation with an inability to establish other supportive relationships after the death of a significant person.

- Concurrent development of physical illness in the survivor, thus causing difficulty with both feelings related to the loss of others and the self.

- "Religious conflict" which leads to suppression of feelings.

- The dead person having extracted a "promise" that the survivor will not be sad or grieve after his or her death.

- Excessive attachment and maintenance of close proximity to possessions of the deceased individual, allowing the survivor to maintain a sense that the deceased is still alive.

- Excessive and premature involvement in life activities to the point that the loss is not acknowledged (pp. 116-117).

Could you provide some examples of how you use this framework to assist you in assessing complicated grief?

Perhaps three separate illustrations of actual persons will be helpful. All three examples are provided in their original dictated form with the exception of names, dates, and locations (changed to insure protection of identities).

Please note that these case presentations also illustrate an overlapping of different complicators and primary catagories of complicated grief.

CASE PRESENTATION A: Susan Johnson
(Date of Consultation: 8-29-86)

I was asked to see this 35-year-old white female, LPN, mother of two children, ages 8 and 6, from the suburbs of Chicago, Illinois. She is currently a patient in the Alcohol and Drug Dependency Unit in General Hospital. She was self-referred for treatment of alcohol and drug abuse. The referral for consultation comes from her primary physician. The content of this report will focus specifically on a assessment of Mrs. Johnson's grief following the death of her father (3-9-83) and her mother (3-2-86).

Throughout the one hour interview Mrs. Johnson appeared to consciously repress any emotional content connected to the death of her parents. She does appear to have insight into the fact that she consciously represses the emotions connected with the sense of loss following the death of her parents, however, she feels "helpless" in terms of being able to express her thoughts and feelings at an emotional level as opposed to an intellectual level. What became obvious immediately was that Mrs. Johnson's experiences with the death of both of her parents in recent years have become complicated by a number of factors that indicate the prognosis of a difficult journey through her grief. The thought is that the most helpful way to be of assistance will be to indicate those areas thought to be complicating factors, and to explore the possibility of short term bereavement therapy.

Complicating Factors
Related To The Death Itself

While Mrs. Johnson was aware that her father had "heart trouble" his death came suddenly and unexpectedly, thus not allowing adequate time for a full psychological preparation. She also expresses some subjective sense of having "participated" in her father's death in that she was aware that he had been ill, had urged him to seek medical care, but had not really forced him to receive medical care. An underlying theme is that she has a sense of responsibility regarding not having done all she could do for her father. She recognizes that she had more time to psychologically prepare herself for her mother's death, however, due to the numbing effects of her chemical dependency she is aware that she avoided the emotions connected to this experience. She appears to have a good sense of having assisted her mother during the process of her illness.

Complicating Factors Related
To Survivor's Psychological Traits

Mrs. Johnson appears to have an extreme dependency on the reflected appraisal of others and the need for excessive approval by those significant people in her life. This appeared to be particularly true in her relationship with her father. While she was separated from him by physical distance, she appears to have maintained a sense of emotional support and strength over the years by receiving his approval. As she speaks what is obvious is that she received more of a personal sense of emotional support in her relationship with her father than she has ever received in her relationship with her husband. She described herself as being her father's "pet". Both her chemical dependency as well as her inherent personality characteristics have made expressing and managing her feelings very difficult regarding sadness, anger, hurt, pain, and loneliness. She stated that she did not grieve for approximately one year following the death of her father in that she felt angry at him for neglecting medical care. She stated that she has continually attempted to convince herself that she did not miss him. An important dynamic in the management of her grief has been her tendency to form an ambivalent relationship with her father whom she states she has both loved and hated. She stated that her hating him relates to his not seeking appropriate medical care. In actuality, a portion of this is a projection of her own sense of not having forced her father to attain medical care. Her inherent psychological traits to inhibit and repress the emotions connected with loss were exacerbated by her chemical dependency.

Complicating Factors Related To The Survivor's Relationship With The Lost Persons

Mrs. Johnson had an extreme dependency particularly on her father for validation of self, identity, and meaning-related activities. As she described her relationship with her father it become apparent that her father was mutually dependent upon her for his own sense of identity. The well modulated anger that she expresses toward her father for not having sought medical assistance appears to be a displacement of her own personal sense of "responsibility" for not having prevented his death. This sense of unresolved conflict in her relationship with her father has served to inhibit her grief response. Her sense of identification with her father seemed to be heightened by their shared mutual interest in the pursuit of music as well as their love for children. The primary loss indicated by her father's death has been a subjective sense of a loss of emotional support in the face of any stressors. Her response has been withdrawal from living, viewing life as threatening and providing only an increased chance of loss of other relationships and the self. She has demonstrated all the classic signs of depressed mood, disruption of interpersonal relationships, loss of interest in life's activities, restlessness, fatigue and exhaustion, varying levels of recognition and acceptance of the loss, a sense of disordered life circumstances, and a subjective feeling of emptiness. She has an extremely difficult time correlating her history of symptoms and chemical dependency to her complicated grief particularly as it relates to her father.

Complicating Factors Related To The Inability To Express Feelings Related To The Losses

Mrs. Johnson is an excellent example of an individual who is unable to be accepting of the high level of feelings surrounding the loss of a person whom she loves. Obviously, her chemical dependency has reinforced the suppression of her feelings. Also a certain component of the suppression of the expression of feelings act as protectiveness toward those around her. She feels that people would certainly not want to hear about her grief and that they would soon grow tired of her personally were she to continue to talk about her mother and father. The talking that she has done has been on a purely intellectual level. She also demonstrates conversion of the expression of grief feelings to unrecognized symbolic expressions. This appears to have been presented at times in terms of identification symptoms involving the physical symptoms that both her mother and father exhibited during their period of illness.

In summary, Mrs. Johnson presents as having components of distorted grief, converted grief, and absent grief particularly as they relate to the death of her father. Her inherent personality characteristics as well as her chemical dependency have served to complicate her grief response. In speaking of her father she also refers to him in the present tense as if he is still alive and living. My impression is that she has an intellectual awareness of both her mother and father's deaths. The anticipatory nature of her mother's death appears to have aided her in an emotional working through of her thoughts and feelings. However, her chemical dependency has been the major inhibiting factor in her ability to mourn both deaths. Obviously much more work needs to be done in assisting her to mourn for her father's death. She appears to be an appropriate candidate for short term re-grief therapy. I will work in consultation with her referring physician to assist her in her reconciliation process.

CASE PRESENTATION B: Robert Smith
(Date of Consultation: 9-13-86)

I was asked to see this 37-year old white male, farmer, father of two children, from rural Iowa. He and his present wife, Mary, had been seen by his referring psychiatrist for conjoint marital therapy on three occasions during the past one month. The purpose of the present consultation was to assess the potential of complicated grief response in Mr. Smith.

Throughout the one hour interview Mr. Smith responded openly to questions regarding the death of his first wife Sally. Mr. Smith's subjective perception is that he has "worked through" the grief related to the death of his first wife. He openly resented the implication that he was in need of grief therapy prior to working on the present relationship with his wife in a marital therapy situation. An undercurrent of a sense of uncertainty was obvious regarding his subjective perception that he has "worked through" his grief. He appeared to be seeking total and complete reassurance that he has dealt with his grief and that no need exists to share his grief with those around him. What became obvious immediately was that Mr. Smith's experience with the death of his first wife was complicated by a number of factors that indicate a complicated grief response. The thought is that the most helpful way to be of assistance will be to indicate those areas thought to be complicating factors, and to initiate short-term bereavement therapy prior to re-initiating marital therapy with his present wife, Mary.

Complicating Factors Related To The Death Itself

Mr. Smith's wife died in a farm accident wherein she had been riding on a tractor which he was driving. She fell off the tractor and incurred massive internal injuries from a piece of equipment that was being pulled by the tractor. She was 33 years of age at the time of her death and had been married to Mr. Smith for 12 years. The sudden and unexpected nature of her death created a situation for Mr. Smith where he had inadequate time for psychological preparation. In addition, he had a sense of having "participated" in the actual event causing the death in that he was driving the tractor at the time of the accident. He does appear to have gone through an extended period of time of obsessionally reviewing how he may have contributed to her death. He does appear to have worked this through a great deal on his own, however, he has never externalized his reconciliation of understanding regarding his culpability in the accident.

Complicating Factors Related To The Survivor's Psychological Traits

Mr. Smith described a mutually dependent relationship with his first wife. He stated "we did everything together." Due to the nature of the farm work they had an opportunity to work side-by-side 24 hours a day for a number of years. Naturally, they grew very close during this period of time, and he expressed very firmly that they made decisions together, never in isolation. Mr. Smith admits to difficulties in giving himself permission to openly express feelings of sadness, anger, hurt, pain, and frustration regarding the loss of his first wife. His difficulty in expressing his emotions was further complicated by his premature re-marriage nine months following the death of his first wife to a woman whom he felt could meet his emotional needs in the same manner in which his wife did. As a consequence, he soon discovered that he could not give himself permission nor receive permission from his present wife regarding the expression of his many thoughts and feelings related to the death of his first wife. His new wife appeared to nurture and support him in the early phases of their relationship and he admits that this in many ways met his needs to be cared for. I would suspect that his failure to establish an independent existence has been undermined to some extent by his present wife who was apparently somewhat threatened by any signs of independence on his part. The rules that they established in their relationship stated that she was to nurture and he was to be supported. Anytime these rules were broken they both became very threatened and as a consequence began to drift apart. He obviously missed the shared lifestyle of farming that he had with his first wife, however, Mary was unfamiliar with farming and was unable to immediately step in and share in this kind of life with him. While Mr. Smith did not consciously feel as if he was attempting to replace his first wife as he is able to look back on the situation more objectively now he realizes this was very much the case.

Complicating Factors Related To The
Survivor's Relationship With The Lost Person

Mr. Smith appeared to have an intensely close relationship with his first wife to the exclusion of very many close relationships with others. To a great extent he had an extreme dependency on her for validation of self, identity, and meaning-related activities. On occasion, he was unable to see himself as a separate person. In some regards he has demonstrated excessive and continued reliance on established life patterns with the pretense of a continued relationship with his first wife.

Complicating Factors Related To The
Inability To Express Feelings
Related To The Loss

In that Mr. Smith prematurely involved himself in a new marital relationship unconsciously in an effort to avoid the many natural feelings of loss related to the death of his first wife he set himself up for a number of complications related to this area. What appears is that both he and Mary have been unable to be accepting of the high levels of feelings surrounding the loss of Sally. On many occasions he has appeared to suppress the expression of his feelings as an act of protectiveness towards Mary. In addition she appears to have communicated to him that she is very threatened by any expression of his emotions related to the death of Sally. The interpersonal disruption of Mr. Smith's life as a consequence of his premature marriage has disallowed the reconciliation of his grief. He has isolated himself in his grief response and has not shared his many thoughts and feelings with anyone around him. Anniversary occasions, birthdays, etc. have been very difficult periods of time for Mr. Smith, however, he has continued to attempt to repress his grief on those occasions for fear of hurting his present wife.

In summary, Mr. Smith has been struggling with a complicated grief reaction that has components of absent, distorted, and converted grief. His premature re-marriage has been a major complicating factor in the journey through his grief. His present wife has felt very insecure in relationship to any expression of his feelings regarding his discussion about his first wife. During the four years of their marriage they appear to have continually been drifting apart as a consequence of both of them feeling very threatened, insecure, and uncertain of how the future would evolve. I explained to Mr. Smith that he does in fact have a complicated grief response. However, I assured him that with some brief psychotherapy focusing on the issues related to his grief that he and his wife could be re-involved in marital therapy with the hope of continuing to work on their relationship. I will see the two of them together for one session and use primarily an educational model related to grief to aid them in their understanding of the external circumstances which have complicated their marital relationship. I will then see Mr. Smith for two brief psychotherapy sessions focusing of the grief which he has internalized. Should I find that he is able to move toward reconciliation I will then suggest that both he and his present wife re-enter marital therapy with their primary therapist.

CASE PRESENTATION C: Debbie White
(Date of Consultation 12-2-85)

This 51-year-old widow was referred by her pastor to the Center For Loss for evaluation and treatment of depression and numerous somatic complaints. Multiple stressors in her life include the sudden and unexpected death of her husband 1½ years ago in Brazil (heart attack), the sudden and unexpected death of her first born son in March of this year in Florida (airplane accident), and her mother's CVA (cerebrovascular accident) three months ago. The content of this report will focus specifically on complicating factors related to Mrs. White's capacity to mourn.

Throughout the one-hour interview Mrs. White appeared to speak very openly at an intellectual level in describing the deaths of her husband and son. On occasion she presented as inappropriately jovial in relating the circumstances and events surrounding these deaths. What became obvious immediately was that Mrs. White's recent experiences with death are complicated by a number of factors which indicate the prognosis of a difficult journey through her grief. The thought is that the most helpful way to be of assistance will be to indicate those areas thought to be complicating factors, and to explore the possibility of short term bereavement therapy.

**Complicating Factors Related
To The Death Itself**

Both recent deaths experienced by Mrs. White are marked by their suddenness, thus not allowing adequate time for psychological preparation. She also speaks of the incomprehensible nature of the deaths, with her husband being in the Amazon, isolated from any chance of the availability of life-saving measures, and her son being killed in a freak accident. Due to the unusual circumstances surrounding both of the deaths, a certain ambiguity and unsureness is in her mind regarding the actual occurrence of these deaths. With her husband's death this relates mostly to the location of the death, and in her son's death, this relates to the unusual nature of the death and her felt sense of physical distance from the actual death. Her absence and isolation from the occurrences surrounding her son's death resulted in inadequate sensory perception for the acknowledgement of its reality. This was also exacerbated by the decision to cremate her son's body immediately after the death, without the opportunity to view his remains. The death of her husband in the Amazon also was complicated by a language barrier, increasing her sense of isolation from the experience. An additional complicating factor related to the death of her husband is her felt sense of having "participated" in the actual event causing the death accompanied by excessive guilt. At the time of his acute MI (myocardial infraction) she attempted to administer CPR for which she has had no training and feels she may have contributed to his death. She also stated that two weeks prior to his death that he stated that he would have a heart attack if things did not change in his life. Furthermore, she feels a test could have predicted his heart problems, therefore preventing his death. She describes it as her responsibility to have known about this test and seen to it that he participated in the evaluation.

Complicating Factors Related To The Survivor's Psychological Traits

Previous projective testing suggests Mrs. White has obsessive-compulsive and dependent personality traits of long standing duration. She admits to difficulty in expressing and managing feelings of sadness and anger. She also appears to be extremely dependent on the reflected appraisals of others, and to have the need for excessive approval by others. Also an apparent tendency is to assume inappropriate levels of responsibility and the presence of excessive guilt over her perceived failure to prevent her husband's death. Also a history exists of excessive dependency on others to meet needs based on a felt sense of limited personal resources. She stated, "I lost more than my son, I lost my creativity." In reference to her husband she stated that she was totally dependent on him and "He made all my decisions for me." Related to the above is Mrs. White's sense of limited options in terms of developing a new lifestyle separate from her husband and son. In addition, she stated that her surviving children feel she is too dependent on them; however, it sounds as if they feel a sense of responsibility to her and probably reinforce her dependency.

Complicating Factors Related To The Survivor's Relationship With The Dead Persons

As previously mentioned, apparently extreme levels of identi-fication exist with both her husband and son. In reference to her husband she stated that they grew closer and closer as their marriage progressed, particularly after all of the children left home. He also was apparently very dependent on her. She stated that she "tucked him in each night." She went on to say that she filled the "motherly" role for him, and he filled the "fatherly" role for her. Furthermore, she stated that, "For 30 years I was my husband's appendage. I clung to my husband and my son. I have lost a sense of being that I had through my son and my husband. I have never lived for myself." Obviously an extreme dependency existed on both her husband and her son for a validation of self, identity, and meaningfully related activities—an inability to see herself as a separate person. She described her son as the "special child" and spoke of their plans to write a book together. She saw her son as much like herself and appears to have experienced vacarious satisfaction of her needs for achievement through her son's accomplishments.

Complicating Factors Related To
The Inability To Express Feelings
Related To The Deaths

Mrs. White appears to have an inability to be accepting of the high levels of feelings surrounding the trauma of the deaths. While some of this could be considered a natural defense mechanism, apparently what exists is an active suppression of the expression of feelings as an act of protectiveness toward others and herself. This is exacerbated by some family members' apparent inability to legitimize and give her permission to experience the full spectrum of feelings related to her grief. Several times she referred to "my daughter, the strong one" indicating that she sees the repression of feelings as an admirable quality. At the time of her husband's death she experienced a sense of dislocation from an interpersonal context that would have been supportive of any expression of feelings. Unfortunately she was given a sedative immediately following his death and this appears to have heightened her sense of dislocation and alienation. She appears to recognize her conversion of the expression of grief feelings to symbolic expressions. She recognizes her periodic heart palpitations as an identification response to her husband and her numerous head-related complaints as an identification with her son. She explains this by stating that some thought about her son was that he was beheaded in the accident. In terms of the heart palpitations, she is aware that she has a mitral valve prolapse; however, she has been reassured that she is in no danger of a heart attack. In addition, she also stated that on occasion she lies in a prone position and appears to associate this with being close to death. Finally, I would mention her excessive and premature involvement in the pursuit of a career in art to the point that the significant emotional impact of the deaths are not acknowledged. Naturally, these intense and extreme losses within a short period of time also have complicated her response.

While the content of this report may seem to point to a poor prognosis, no reason is evident why with proper support and guidance, Mrs. White should not be able to experience her grief and move in the direction of reconciliation. However, one would want to keep in mind her predisposing personality factors which served to complicate her present situation. Her pastor would like me to assume her care at this time and I have agreed to do so. He will remain involved as an important support system for her.

Summary

Clearly, the distinction between "normal grief" and "complicated" grief is difficult at best. In summary, we have noted that complicated grief is often a distortion or conversion of the expected mourning process. Extensive guidelines for the treatment of complicated grief is beyond the scope of this book. The reader interested in additional information is referred to the references at the conclusion of this section.

Bereaved persons should be encouraged to seek help in understanding the expression, or lack of expression of their experiences with grief. When in doubt about the "normalcy"of some phenomenon, the wise procedure is to seek out assistance. Getting help for oneself is a reflection of self-care, not testimony that one is "crazy."

How do I respond to members of my church who ask me if I think they need help with their grief?

First, their asking the question is usually an indicator of their awareness of a need to seek out supportive guidance. Secondly, I would suggest attempting to discover their perception of the following questions:

Does their grief interfere with the ability to care for self and the capacity to find life meaningful?

Do they find that they consistently withdraw from people and life in general?

Do they have physical and emotional symptoms that they do not understand?

Do they suffer from distorted feelings of anger, guilt, or any others dimension of grief?

Have they noticed changes in their personalities that they cannot seem to control?

Do they have an internal sense that they are not healing in the experience of their grief?

If they answer yes to any of these questions, you would be wise to supportively encourage their seeking out some form of professional guidance.

REFERENCES

[1]   Lazare, A. (1979). Unresolved grief. In A. Lazare (Ed.), *Outpatient psychiatry: Diagnosis and treatment.* Baltimore: Williams & Wilkins.

[2]   Freud, S. (1957). Mourning and melancholia. In *Standard Edition of Complete Psychological Works of Sigmund Freud,* (Vol. 14). London: Hogarth Press.

[3]   Lindemann, E. (1944). Symptomotology and management of acute grief. *American Journal of Psychiatry. 101,* 141-148.

[4]   Bowlby J. (1980). Loss, sadness and depression. Vol. 3. In *Attachment and loss.* London: Hogarth Press.

[5]   Siggins, L.D. (1966). Mourning: a critical survey of the literature. *International Journal of Psychoanalysis, 47,* 14-25.

[6]   Welu, T.C. (1975). Preventing pathological bereavement. In B. Schoenbert et al. (Eds.), *Bereavement: Its psychosocial aspects.* New York: Columbia University Press.

[7]   DeVaul, R.A. & Zisook, S. (1976). Unresolved grief. *Postgraduate Medicine. 59,* 5.

8 Averill, J.R. (1968). Grief: Its nature and significance. *Psychological Bulletin, 70,* 721-748.

9 Parkes, L.M., & Weiss, R.S. (1983). *Recovery from bereavement.* New York: Basic Books.

10 Raphael, B. (1983). The anatomy of bereavement. New York: Basic Books.

11 Worden, J.W. (1982). *Grief counseling and grief therapy: A handbook for the mental health practitioner.* New York: Springer.

12 Rando, T.A. (1981). *Grief dying and death: Clinical interventions for caregivers.* Champaigne, IL: Research Press.

13 Lifton, R.J. (1976). The sense of immortality: On death and the continuity of life. In R. Fulton (Ed.), *Death and identity.* Bowie, MD: The Charles Press.

14 Barton, D. (1977). The process of grief. In D. Barton (Ed.), *A clinical guide for caregivers.* Baltimore: Williams and Wilkins.

12
DURATION OF GRIEF

I have heard a variety of time frames given for the duration of grief. How long do you think grief lasts?

As one widow stated five years after the death of her husband, "Mourning never ends; only as time goes on it erupts less frequently."[1] Each person has a different time frame for working toward reconciliation. Those factors that influence a person's individual response (see pages 25-32) will have a significant impact on the journey through grief.

As a reminder, included among those factors are the following:

1. the nature of the relationship with the person who dies;

2. the availability, helpfulness, and ability of the person to make use of a social support system;

3. the unique characteristics of the bereaved person;

4. the unique characteristics of the person who died;

5. the nature of the death;

6. the person's religious and cultural history;

7. other crisis or stresses in the person's life;

8. previous experience with death;

9. the social expectations based on the sex of the survivor; and

10. the ritual or funeral experience.

The majority of mourners, as well as caregivers have unrealistic expectations of the ease and speed at which the bereaved person should "get over" the grief. A theme of this book is that one does not "get over" grief, but instead works to "live with" and reconcile his or her grief. We have already outlined (see pages 3-5) how the lack of a supportive social context influences peoples perception that grief is something to be overcome rather than experienced. We stated that many grieving people have internalized society's message that grief should be done quietly and quickly.

Some researchers have attempted to set definitive dates as to when mourning should be completed. The results are often misleading and inconclusive. Problems are inherent in the very nature of the research. For example, a person might be interviewed at one point in the experience of grief and respond that he or she is having few, if any, symptoms. Then, interviewed even a week or several months later and then report extensive distress. This wave-like quality to the experience is very common. A transition to another dimension of mourning may bring a renewal of normal signs and symptoms of acute grief. Furthermore, a number of studies are misleading in that they only follow the bereaved person for a specific period of time, typically two years. Obviously, this time span makes generalized statement about the specific length of mourning impossible to make.

Perhaps the most effective way to determine the mourners movement toward reconciliation is to assess what was previously termed "needs of reconciliation" or tasks of mourning (see pages 73-81). Acknowledging the impossibility of setting a particular time frame, I will share with you that my clinical experience has been that the majority of mourners need between two to three years to work through these needs of reconciliation. Again, simply as a reminder, included among the five needs of reconciliation outlined in this text are the following:

1. to experience and express outside of oneself the reality of the death,

2. to tolerate the emotional suffering that is inherent in the work of grief while nurturing oneself both physically and emotionally,

3. to convert the relationship with the deceased from one of presence to a relationship of memory,

4. to develop a new self-identity based on a life without the deceased, and

5. to relate the experience of loss to a context of meaning.

Despite how effectively the work on these needs of reconciliation is done, the process cannot be collapsed in time. Anniversaries, holidays, birthdays and other significant occasions in the life of the family will usually bring a resurgence of intense feelings of loss and sadness. To acknowledge and embrace these feelings is healthier than to attempt to repress and deny them. Unfortunately, some people will attempt to repress these feelings out of a felt need to demonstrate to self and others that he or she is over the grief. However, while the physical person is gone, memories and natural feelings of sadness on special occasions live on. As a helper, you have the opportunity to assist people in embracing these memories as opposed to repressing or denying them.

In summary, people are forever changed by the experience of death in their lives. We, as humans, do not "get over" our grief, but work to reconcile ourselves to living with it. Anyone who attempts to prescribe a specific time-frame for the experience only creates another barrier to the healing process.

REFERENCES

[1] Bowlby, J. (1980). *Attachment and loss: Loss, sadness, and depression, Vol. 3.* New York: Basic Books.

NOTES

13

ANNIVERSARY REACTIONS

I know of several parishioners in my church who had had a resurgence of grief on anniversary occasions of the death of their spouse. Could you comment on the phenomenon of anniversary reactions?

Naturally, anniversary occasions result in a renewed sense of grief. Birthdays; wedding dates; holidays such as Easter, Thanksgiving, and Christmas; and other special occasions create a focus for the sense of loss that results in a change in behavior and feelings on these dates.

A renewed grief experience may occur not only in response to specific anniversaries, but also in response to circumstances which serve to remind consciously the mourner of the death. For many families certain times had special meaning related to family togetherness and the person is more deeply missed at those times. For example, the onset of spring, the first snow, an annual Fourth of July party, or anytime when activities were done together as a family.

The major task for the mourner is to accept and work to survive the naturalness of these anniversary reactions. Many people well describe the anticipation of the anniversary as sometimes being worse than the day itself. This phenomenon speaks of the need to plan ahead in anticipation of this more vulnerable period of time. Unfortunately, some mourners will not mention anniversaries to people around them suffering in silence and increasing their sense of isolation on these days. Taking inventory of a bereaved persons anniversary occasions allows support to be provided as those times occur.

Caregivers can be instrumental in helping organize meaningful activities to mark the anniversary or other special occasions.

For example, services can be held that provide a forum for their expression of thoughts and feelings on these days. Some religions have ceremonies that provide for this structured expression of grief. Other useful activities might include taking flowers to the grave of the person who died, looking at old photos, or having a special dinner for close friends and family. The purpose of these activities is to legitimize the need to talk about and have memories of the dead person.

In my experience, without some avenue for expression during these difficult times, the person is likely to experience the "going crazy syndrome." The planning and sharing of sadness can serve as a catalyst for continued healing.

14
GRIEF AVOIDANCE RESPONSE STYLES

You have made reference on several occasions to how mourners sometimes adopt what you term "grief avoidance response styles." Could you define what these are and how they are expressed in terms of behavior?

While a number of unique ways occur by which persons repress or "move away" from the expression of their grief, we can work to identify common patterns that are adopted[1]. The various patterns of avoiding grief described in this section are not mutually exclusive. Some people will experience a combination of patterns while others will maintain one primary mode of avoidance. The specific combination of patterns (or primary mode used most often) will depend on one's personal history, societal influences, and basic personality.

The destructive effect of the adopted pattern is typically directly proportional to the degree of avoidance. However, prolonged avoidance, whatever the degree, will always be destructive. In moving away from our feelings of grief, that is, in repressing, denying, or deadening our feelings, we ultimately become destructive to ourselves. Our refusal to do the "work of mourning" destroys much of our capacity to enjoy life, living, and loving. After all, how can we relate to ourselves or others if we don't feel? Moving away from grief results in moving away from ourselves and other people.

The avoidance patterns identified and described in this section are as follows:

> the postponer,
> the displacer,
> the replacer,
> the minimizer, and
> the somaticizer,

THE POSTPONER

The postponer is the person who believes that if you delay the expression of your grief, over time it will hopefully go away. Obviously, it does not. The grief builds within and typically comes out in a variety of ways that do not best serve the needs of the mourner.

This person may feel that if the grief doesn't vanish, at least at some point in time he or she will feel safer, in experiencing the pain. Unaware that through expression comes healing, he or she continues to postpone. The grief builds up inside the person, pushing toward the point of explosion, thus making him or her feel even less capable of experiencing feelings related to the loss.

Without self-awareness or intervention, a vicious cycle is firmly rooted in place. Often the more the person senses grief yearning for expression, the more an effort is made to postpone or put off.

Postponing is frequently an automatic unconscious process. A few people will consciously acknowledge this pattern with comments like, "I just don't want to grieve right now. I'll think about it later." However, the majority of people do not know they are postponing the work of their grief. They initiate this pattern of avoidance quietly and quickly and society often perceives them as "doing very well."

THE DISPLACER

The displacer is the person who takes the expression of the grief away from the loss itself and displaces the feelings in other directions. For example, while not acknowledging feelings of grief the person may complain of difficulty at work or in relationships with other people. Another example is the person who appears to be chronically agitated and upset at even the most minor of events. While some awareness may be present, displacing usually occurs with total unconsciousness.

Some persons who adopt the displacer orientation, become bitter toward life in general. Others displace the bitter unconscious expression of their grief inward and become full of self-hate and experience debilitating depression. So, while at times these persons displace their grief in interactions with other people, at other times, they believe that other people dislike them, once again projecting unhappiness from the inside to the outside.

The main intent of the displacer is to shift grief away from its sources and onto a less threatening person, place, or situation. Personal relationships often become stressed and strained for the displacer who is unable to acknowledge the occurrence of this common pattern of grief avoidance.

THE REPLACER

The replacer is the person who takes the emotions that were invested in the relationship that ended in death and reinvests the emotions prematurely in another relationship. Again, very little, if any, conscious awareness occurs for these persons of how their replacement efforts are really a means of avoiding the work of their grief.

Observers from the outside will sometimes assume the replacer must not have loved the person that died all that much if they can so quickly become involved in a new relationship. In actuality, the replacer has often loved very much and out of the need to overcome the pain of confronting feelings related to the loss, moves into an avoidance pattern of replacement.

The replacement pattern does not only occur in relationships with other people. For example, another common replacement appears in the person who overworks. The compulsive overworker is the person who, with no prior history of doing so, begins to over invest himself or herself in work to the point where no time is available to think or feel about the loss.

An example of this is a man I recently saw in my practice who, following the death of his wife, found himself working eighteen to twenty house a day. What was apparent was that he was funneling all of the emotions related to his wife's death onto and through his work.

Once this pattern was acknowledged for the need it was serving in him, he could begin to do the work of his mourning in healthy, life-giving ways.

THE MINIMIZER

The minimizer is the person who is aware of feelings of grief, but when felt, works to minimize the feelings by diluting them through a variety of rationalizations. This person attempts to prove to self that he or she is not really impacted by the loss that was experienced. Observers of minimizers may well hear them talk about how they are back to their normal routines.

On a conscious level the minimizer may seem to be working and certainly conforming to society's message to quickly "get over" one's grief. However, internally the repressed feelings of grief build within and emotional strain results.

This person often believes that grief is something to be quickly thought through, but not felt through. This is typically an intellectual process in which words become a substitute for the expression of authentic feelings. Any feelings of grief are very threatening to the minimizer who seeks to avoid pain at all costs.

Unfortunately, the more this person works to convince self that the feelings of grief have been "overcome," the more crippled he or she becomes in allowing for emotional expression. The result is the evolution of a destructive vicious cycle.

THE SOMATICIZER

The somaticizer is the person who converts his or her feelings of grief into physical symptoms. This converted physical expression of grief can range from relatively benign minor complaints to the severely malignant chronic pattern of somaticization disorder, i.e., multiple vague somatic complaints with no organic findings.

Unfortunately many people in grief unconsciously adopt the somaticizer role in an effort to get their emotional needs met. By taking on the "sickrole" people around them legitimize their very real need to be nurtured and comforted. These persons often fear that if they were to express their true feelings of grief that people would pull away and leave them feeling abandoned.

The somaticizer may become so completely preoccupied with bodily involvement and sickness the he or she has little or no energy to relate to others and to do the work of the mourning. Even in the absence of real illness and emotional support from medical caregivers, no amount of reassurance or logic convinces the somaticizer that he or she is not "physically sick." The unconscious need to protect oneself requires that this person desperately needs the belief in illness to mask feelings connected to the death.

We should note that this somaticizer avoidance pattern is different than the person who experiences real physical illness during the mourning process. Some degree of physical disturbance is a common dimension of the normal grief process. As caregivers we would never want to automatically assume that a bereaved person is converting all of his or her emotions into physical symptoms. Numerous investigations have documented a definite physical risk for the griever much greater than that of the nonbereaved population. A general medical examination for bereaved persons is always an excellent standard of care.

Consequences of Adopting
Grief Avoidance Patterns

The specific reasons bereaved people adopt grief avoidance patterns are often multiple and complicated. For the purpose of this book we will simply note that the major impediments to the healthy expression of grief are usually problems in allowing oneself to feel and to express deep feelings. Some people have struggles with a high need for self-control, others may have an intolerance to feelings of pain and helplessness, while still others lack a support system that encourages the expression of their feelings.

The result of grief avoidance is a virtual epidemic of complicated and unreconciled grief in our country. This writer's clinical experience suggests that a tremendous amount of anxiety, depression, and physical illness has resulted from many persons needs to avoid their grief.

Among some of the more common consequences of adopting grief avoidance patterns are the following:

- deterioration in relationships with friends and family;
- symptoms of chronic physical illness either real or imagined;

- symptoms of chronic depression, sleeping difficulties, and low self-esteem; and
- symptoms of chronic anxiety, agitation, restlessness, and difficulty concentrating.

This list is not intended to be all-inclusive. Different people will experience a wide variety of fall-out consequences from their adoption of avoidance patterns.

REFERENCES

[1] Wolfelt, A. (1987). Understanding common patterns of avoiding grief. *Thanatos*, *12*, 2, 2-5.

15

RESPECTING DENIAL

You have made reference to what you termed "respecting denial, yet encouraging emotional expression." What do you mean by this?

I believe that early in the experience of grief part of the caregiver's role is to create an artful balance between encouraging emotional expression and respecting denial. Denial in the sense of the mourner's need to temporarily block out the reality of the death because the pain at that point is overwhelming the person's capacity to cope. The key is that this denial is a temporary means of self-protection that helps the person survive the moment.

This natural defense of denial only becomes an impediment to healing when it becomes fixed or rigid. Typically, an alternating occurs between the testing of reality, "This person I love is really dead," and the survival need to deny, "It can't be, he's not dead." No specific beginning or ending point can be identified to this normal process inherent to the experience of grief. One moment the mourner may speak openly of the reality of the death and the next moment revert to a normal defensive need to employ denial.

While one of the needs of reconciliation is to eventually experience and express the reality of the death, acute grief is a process consisting of these alternating tendencies—one to deny and push away the pain and the other to confirm the reality of the death. Respecting grief as a process that not immediately, but ultimately, leads to a complete recognition of the death is critical to the helping role.

As a caregiver, a need exists to be sensitive to the timing of getting a mourner to fully acknowledge the reality of the death. For example, you can do things that help the person acknowledge the reality, i.e., encouraging them to view the body, without saying, (some well-meaning but uninformed people actually do this) "You just have to accept that he is dead and isn't coming back."

A helpful balance must be struck between comforting mourners while at the same time helping them encounter the new reality. The accomplishment of both of these helping task is much more helpful than doing only one to the exclusion of the other.

16
VIEWING THE BODY
OF THE DECEASED

In your last response you mentioned that viewing the body helps the mourner acknowledge the reality of the death. This seems to be a controversial area of discussion. For example, I'm aware that some people think not viewing the body is best. What are your thoughts on this?

We have observed a trend in recent years away from viewing the body of the person who had died. At the same time our society is claiming to be more open and honest about death. Some of the changes in traditions we are witnessing are actually creating an upsurge in complicated grief responses. My own clinical experience suggests that this trend away from viewing the body frequently makes for more difficulty in accomplishing the work of the first reconciliation need outlined in this text (To Experience and Express Outside of Oneself the Reality of the Death).

The first reconciliation need of the mourner is to acknowledge the reality of the death; to break through the conflicting desire to push away the encounter with the new reality. The delicate balance between the wish to avoid reality while needing to confront the reality is assisted by the rituals we have evolved since the beginning of time. Viewing the body is a practice that has existed since time immemorial. Seeing the body challenges the natural wish to avoid the reality of the death. While, at the same time, encouraging healthy acceptance of the death.

Raphael[1] provided an excellent summary that is in agreement with my own thoughts on this issue:

> All evidence suggests that seeing the body of the dead person is an important part of the adjustment process: it provides an opportunity to see and become familiar with the realities of death; it is an opportunity to

see and touch, for the last tenderness, for the last goodbye; perhaps hold the dearly loved one for the last time. Unfortunately many medical and legal systems, as well as well-meaning others may intrude to prevent this from happening or may limit it, thus frustrating its adaptive function for the bereaved. In many instances the bereaved may only be allowed to view the body through a screen, or not be allowed to touch it, or, very often, not be allowed to hold it. There may be no opportunity for a private time with the dead person—a time for reminiscence and regret, sadness and farewell. The experience of seeing and saying goodbye to the dead person as a dead person makes it possible for the bereaved to develop the image of the person as dead, different and altered from the living image. This image may be held alongside the living image in the process of separation and mourning. (pp. 35-36)

A natural ambivalence is experienced by most persons surrounding the viewing of the body. How many of you have overheard, or perhaps told yourself, "I just want to remember him the way he was when he was alive." While this is a normal wish, it is most often directed at self-protection away from having to experience the painful responses that result from acknowledging the reality of the death.

As strange as it may seem, the bereaved person's mind requires evidence that the person is no longer living. The opportunity to view the body provides this evidence. You might hear someone say, "But I don't want the picture of my dead husband to be the lasting image in my mind." Experience suggests that the dead image will not be the forever lasting image in the mind of the survivor. While it is the image of the person being dead that allows for the verification of the death, that very image usually fades and the living memories become everlasting.

When a sense of isolation occurs from the events surrounding the death, or, the death is sudden and unexpected, viewing the body becomes even more important. When the death has been sudden or survivors have been unable to be in close proximity to the dead person during the dying process it becomes more difficult for the mourner to convince self that the person has actually died. Perhaps an example would help here.

I was recently consulted by a funeral home that was having difficulty in working with a particular family. A 16-year-old boy had died suddenly in a tragic automobile accident. The boy's father was refusing to come into the funeral home to make funeral arrangements. The father had been informed that he would be unable to view his son's body due to the extent of the injuries. The father had convinced himself of the following: "My son is not dead. Someone stole his car and that is actually who died. My son had talked about going away to California. I'm just sure that is where he is right now."

My recommendation to the funeral home was that under these circumstances the father would have to be allowed and encouraged to see his son's body. While difficult, restorative work was done on the body and the father was able to view a portion of his son's body. At that point he was gently and supportively forced to confront the brutal reality of his son's death and the funeral arrangements proceeded. Following the funeral he said to the funeral director who helped the family, "You know, I really didn't believe it would be my son. But, when I saw him I could no longer convince myself otherwise. Thank you for making it possible to see him, touch him, and hold him one last time.

As indicated in this example, the tendency to avoid the reality of a death becomes heightened when the nature of the death is sudden and unexpected. Yet, the need to confirm reality becomes even more critical during these times. Allowing for and encouraging the viewing of the body allows the work of grief to move in a helpful direction. Any attempts to avert the first reconciliation need (acknowledging the reality of the death) often results in the beginning of a complicated grief response.

REFERENCES

[1]   Raphael, B. (1983). *The anatomy of bereavement.* New York: Basic Books.

NOTES

17

FUNCTION OF TEARS

What function does crying play in the expression of feelings of grief?

Unfortunately, some people associate tears of grief with personal inadequacy and weakness. Crying on the part of the mourner often generates feelings of helplessness in friends, family, and caregivers. Out of a wish to protect the mourner from pain those people surrounding the mourner may serve to inhibit the experience of tears. Comments similar to, "Tears won't bring him back", and, "He wouldn't want you to cry" discourage the expression of tears. Crying also can be defended against by bereaved persons themselves.

Yet, crying is natures way of releasing internal tension in the body and allows the mourner to communicate a need to be comforted. Another function of crying is postulated in the context of attachment theory[1] wherein tears are intended to bring about reunion with the lost person. While the reunion cannot occur, crying is thought to be biologically based and a normal way of attempting to reconnect with the person who has died. The frequency and intensity of crying eventually wanes as the hoped for reunion does not occur.

While research in this area is still limited, some investigators have suggested that suppressing tears may increase susceptability to stress-related disorders. This would seem to make sense in that crying is an exocrine process—one of the excretory processes. In reviewing other excretory processes, such as sweating, exhaling, and urinating, the fact is that they all involve the removal of waste product from the body. Crying may serve a similar function.

In my clinical experience with thousands of mourners I have observed changes in physical expressions following the expression of tears. While this is purely a subjective observation, seemingly not only do people feel better after crying, they also look better.

Expressions of tension and agitation seem to flow out of their body. The capacity to express tears appears to allow for a genuine catharsis.

Another clinical observation is that the majority of mourners need help in exploring the meaning of their tears. The meaning of tears often changes as the mourner works toward reconciliation. Whereas at one point early in grief tears might be expressive of acute pain resulting from the loss, at another time, tears may be expressive of the joy of having the opportunity to embrace memories of the deceased. While you as a helper would not be wise to attempt to directly interpret the meaning of tears for the mourner, you can create opportunities for silence, and a supportive presence that allows the mourner to provide his or her own meaning. The capacity of the mourner to share tears with you is an indication of the willingness to enter into the work of mourning. The sharing of tears with you is also an opportunity to provide the mourner with a sense of feeling understood, which is at the core of all effective counsel.

REFERENCES

[1] Glick, I.O., Weiss, R.S., & Parkes, C.M. (1974). *The first year of bereavement.* New York: Jason Aronson.

18

BEREAVEMENT OVERLOAD

I have heard the term "bereavement overload." What does this mean?

Kastenbaum[1] has used the term bereavement overload to describe the experience of suffering too many deaths with a certain period of time. The term applies equally well to the mourner, the caregiver, and, at times, the nation as a whole. Examples of each follow.

Bereavement Overload for the Mourner

I recently worked with a family where the mother shot and killed the father and was subsequently sentenced to prison. The four children experienced: (1) the tragic death of their father, (2) the loss of their mother to imprisonment, (3) separation from each other through placement in three separate homes, (4) loss of some previous supportive family relationships, and (5) changes in schools attended. Obviously, the death of their father resulted in bereavement overload for these children.

Bereavement Overload for the Caregiver

During this past year, a clergy friend of mine experienced the death of 18 parishioners in his church. After officiating at 24 funerals he would certainly meet the criteria for bereavement overload.

Bereavement Overload for the Nation

The explosion of the space shuttle Challenger was certainly an example of bereavement overload for the nation. Another example was when the nation experienced the deaths of John Kennedy, Martin Luther King, and Robert Kennedy all within a short period of time.

The original use of the term was used to refer to the series of losses experienced by older persons in later life. Bereavement overload is a natural complicator to the experiences of grief and requires that special attention be paid to the needs of the mourner.

REFERENCES

[1] Kastenbaum, R.J. (1969). Death and bereavement in later life. In A.H. Kutsher (Ed.), *Death and bereavement,* Springfield, IL: Charles C. Thomas.

19
ANTICIPATORY GRIEF

I would like for you to define the term "anticipatory grief[1]." I hear it used a lot, but I'm not sure I know what it is. What is it?

Anticipatory grief[1] is typically used to mean any grief occurring prior to a loss; as distinguished from the grief which occurs at or after the loss. Kübler-Ross's classic text *On Death and Dying*[2] described the anticipatory grief process of the dying patient, or "patient anticipatory grief"; however, the term is typically used to describe the experience of families of the terminally ill, or "family anticipatory grief."

Historically, investigators of this concept of anticipatory grief thought that prolonged illness helped prepare survivors for the death in ways that eased the grief when the death actually occurred. However, more recent studies[3] [4] [5] have suggested that the grief experienced after an anticipated loss is no less painful than when loss is not anticipated. However, these investigators did observe that the process of anticipatory grief does allow for less of an assault on the mourner's adaptive capacities. Fulton and Gottesman[6] have suggested that anticipatory grief has at times been confused with what they term "forewarning of loss." These and other studies reinforce the need for additional research to help us better understand this phenomenon.

To date, the best comprehensive understanding of anticipatory grief is provided in the text, *Loss and Anticipatory Grief*[7]. This text sensitively illustrates how this phenomenon is more complex and impacted by more factors than previously considered. Among topics included in the contents are a review of current literature on the topic, clinical interventions, developmental issues, and practical considerations. Those readers wishing to obtain a more in-depth understanding of anticipatory grief are urged to read the text by T.A. Rando.

My own clinical experience would suggest that anticipatory grief is experienced differently by different families. Therefore, to generalize about how this process manifests itself in the dynamics of the family becomes difficult, if not impossible. For example, during the period of anticipatory grief I have worked with some families who had difficulty maintaining their involvement in the care of the dying person. This seems to occur when they have worked to "let go" of their dying family member, and having done so, find it difficult to continue to invest in aspects of care that they perceive as prolonging the inevitable—death.

However, at the other end of the spectrum, I have worked with families where a heightened attachment during a long period of illness seems to have emotionally disallowed anticipatory grief from occurring. Shuchter[8] provides an excellent real-life vignette from the San Diego Widowhood Project:

> Melinda's struggle with Jim's cancer intensified their relationship in many ways. Melinda became inseparable from Jim physically, attending to his moment-to-moment needs on a twenty-four-hour-per-day basis, nursing him with greater degrees of intimacy and greater exposure to his most private moments. At the same time she fought furiously to deny his illness, to preserve hope, and to maintain a positive spirit. All these actions conspired to make their relationship more real to her and deeper than it had ever been.

> During the years after the onset of his illness and before his death, David and Carol became much closer. They talked about all aspects of living and dying, and they got to know each other's innermost thoughts and feelings in a way that they never had before. "We had a much deeper communication than we had all of our married life." (pp. 70)

Despite some of the present controversy surrounding the phenomenon of anticipatory grief, we must continue to work toward deepening our understanding of how different families grieve in anticipation of death. Opportunities to assist during this time can help subvert potential complicated grief responses both before and after the moment of death. Regardless of our need for further understanding of anticipatory grief, most people would probably agree that the experience of grief does not begin at the event of death, but when a person enters the transition from being alive and living to dying.

REFERENCES

[1] Aldrich, C.K. (1974). Some dynamics of anticipatory grief. In B. Schoenberg, A. Carr, A. Kutscher, D. Peretz, & I Goldberg (Eds.), *Anticipatory grief.* New York: Columbia University Press.

[2] Kübler-Ross, E. (1969). *On death and dying.* New York: Macmillan.

[3] Parkes, C.M., & Weiss, R.S. (1983). *Recovery from bereavement.* New York: Basic Books.

[4] Glick, I.O., Weiss, R.S., & Parkes, C.M. (1974). *The first year of bereavement.* New York: Wiley.

[5] Clayton, P.J., Halikas, J.A., Maurice, W.H., & Robbins, E. (1973). Anticipatory grief and widowhood. *British Journal of Psychiatry, 122,* 47-51.

[6] Fulton, R., & Gottesman, D.J. (1980). Anticipatory grief: A psychosocial concept reconsidered. *British Journal of Psychiatry, 137,* 45-54.

[7] Rando, T.A. (1986). *Loss and anticipatory grief.* Lexington, MA: Lexington Books.

[8] Shuchter, S.R. (1986). *Dimensions of grief: Adjusting to the death of a spouse.* San Francisco: Josey-Bass Publishers.

NOTES

20

USE OF MEDICATION

What is your thinking on the use of medication with the bereaved person?*

Unfortunately, many people surrounding the mourner, as well as the mourner, are sometimes quick to seek out the use of medication in the treatment of grief. The desire to want to avoid and mask acute pain is understandable, yet to do so only brings temporary relief from an emotional suffering that must be endured.

We have had the unfortunate experience of working with many mourners who were so medicated at the time of the funeral that they have little, if any, memory of the experience. Consequently, these people felt a sense of distance from the reality of the death at precisely the time when the use of ritual could have allowed for the expression of their grief. These experiences have challenged us to work to educate both the medical and lay communities about the appropriate and inappropriate use of medication with mourners.[1]

We often question what is communicated to the mourner when he or she is encouraged to take psychopharmacological agents at a time of grief. In our experience encouraging the mourner to take a medication that is intended to change or alter his or her emotional and physical state communicates that what he or she is feeling is wrong. Yet, as previously outlined, nature has a way of protecting and helping the mourner survive the experience of acute grief. To add an additional numbing effect to an already numbing experience only moves the mourner further away from accomplishing the first reconciliation need (To Experience and Express Outside of Oneself the Reality of the Death), as well as, the second reconciliation need (To Tolerate the Emotional Suffering That is Inherent in the Work of Grief While Nurturing Oneself Both Physically and Emotionally).

Whatever alters the mourner's internal environment to produce temporary numbing effects also has the potential to induce new and additional complications to the grief process. For example, some persons become psychologically and physically dependent on the continued use of medication. The result is a heightened sense of weakness and vulnerability in an already threatening environment. Despite some people's beliefs that you can push feelings away chemically, to prescribe medication during times of acute grief is usually motivated out of a defensive need to protect the mourner and oneself from confronting painful feelings in a direct fashion.

Some people are quick to blame physicians for the indiscriminent use of medication with bereaved people. While the medical profession must share responsibility for this problem, the public also must recognize its own responsibility. Clinical experience suggests that many mourners receive the initial supply of medication (primarily tranquilizers, sedatives, and antidepressants) from well-meaning, but uninformed friends and family members. To place all of the blame at the doorstep of the medical profession is to abdicate self-responsibility from a recurring problem. We also should be careful about blaming the mourner for this problem. After all, the mourner typically becomes naturally passive during acute grief and is therefore vulnerable to the message of people surrounding him or her that often goes something like this, "Here take this, it will make you feel better."

We should also note that alcohol abuse and dependence are also potential problems for the mourner. Not by chance alone has alcohol use and abuse become problems for many bereaved people. Alcohol is perhaps the most common form of self-medication for the bereaved. Many subcultures in our society condone and encourage the use of alcohol during times of bereavement. However, because alcohol use can become psychologically as well as physically addicting, a pattern of continued use and abuse can occur. The result for some is the evolution of a dependent state and the creation of an entirely new set of problems. As the amount of alcohol consumed increases, so too does difficulties with feeling agitated and depressed. In addition, sleeping and eating patterns are negatively impacted.

When alcohol or other drugs take on an abuse or dependence pattern within the mourner, these problems must be addressed before grief reconciliation can occur. Some caregivers will attempt to reverse the process, thinking that if they can assist the mourner with the grief that the other problems will disappear. However, alcohol and drug dependences have a mind of their own that require different intervention and treatment modalities. If you suspect the potential of an alcohol or drug problem, the wise procedure is to arrange for a consultation from a trained drug and alcohol counselor.

The information outlined in this section is not intended to suggest that the use of medication with bereaved people is never appropriate. For example some people become both physically and emotionally exhausted after going a prolonged period of time without sleep. As previously noted it takes energy to do the work of grief. Careful assessment may indicate the need for limited night-time sedation when prolonged insomnia becomes a problem. In addition, other indications may be present to suggest the need for a qualified medical practitioner to assist in the assessment of the potential need for medication. Other examples would include the following: phobic anxiety states, mania, psychosis, and clinical depression.

Perhaps the area where the most misdiagnosis and treatment occurs is with clinical depression and the use of antidepressant medication. We have provided a number of consultations to bereaved people where we have discovered that they were placed on antidepressants during the acute time of their grief. In most situations, no prior history of clinical depression existed and the presenting symptoms were in line with a normal grief response. The chemical action of these medications take a long time to work and they will not relieve normal grief symptoms in a non-clinically depressed person. As a general rule to prescribe antidepressants to mourners experiencing acute grief that have no prior history of clinical depression is unwise. Doing so only sets the mourner up for a more complicated grief response.

The preceding information reinforces the importance of the bereavement caregiver's need to be familiar with the differential diagnosis of normal grief from clinical depression. Some assistance in learning to make this differentiation is provided on page

55. However, when in doubt an excellent standard of care would be to seek assistance from a qualified caregiver in making the distinction.

In summary, loss-related feelings of grief eventually catch up with the mourner at one time or another. While at selective times medications can and should be carefully used with mourners, when possible, the preferred avenue of care is to have support and guidance from a fellow human being for experiencing and expressing feelings of grief. Reconciliation comes through the expression of thoughts and feelings, not through becoming abusive or dependent on drugs of any kind.

REFERENCE

*   The author credits his wife, Susan J. Wolfelt, M.D., with assistance in responding to this question. Dr. Susan J. Wolfelt is the Chief of Staff at Colorado State University Health Center. Board certified in family medicine, she serves as a medical consultant to the Center for Loss and Life Transition.

[1]   Wolfelt, A.D., and Wolfelt, S.J. (Fall, 1987). Medication and the mourner: Understanding a complex issue. *Thanatos, 12:3*, pp. 18-19.

21

FAITH AND THE EXPRESSION OF GRIEF

I have several parishioners in my church who seem to equate having faith with not allowing themselves to grieve. Could you comment on this?

Many people seem to ask the question, "Does having faith mean that one does not grieve?" For some people, it seems that having faith in God and believing in eternal life seems out of step with the open expression of grief; therefore, they repress the natural expression of thoughts and feelings related to the loss. Obviously, this way of thinking is a natural set-up for a complicated grief response. Presbyterian minister, R. Scott Sullender[1] expressed the situation nicely:

> We are accustomed to thinking that if we just had enough faith, we would not have any doubts. Some soldiers are accustomed to thinking that if they just had enough bravery, they would not have any fears in battle. Some grieving people are accustomed to thinking that if they just had enough faith, they would not feel any sorrow. All of these "accustomed" ways of thinking are unhelpful. In contrast, faith as courage suggests that faith is trusting God in spite of one's doubts, that bravery is action in spite of one's fears, and that faith is hope in a new tomorrow in spite of one's present sorrow. Sometimes faith is the courage to trust in spite of feeling to the contrary. (pp. 199)

The mourner may need support and guidance as he or she struggles to explore questions related to death and faith. Encouraging mourners to teach you about their faith in the context of their losses, usually opens up an important area of exploration. Allow persons to teach you such things as

1. whether they feel comforted by their faith or abandoned by their faith,

2. what meaning or value they find in their religions faith or philosophy of life,

3. whether death means eternal life or the final end,

4. whether they perceive the cause of death to be from divine or natural causes,

5. what relationships do they see existing between death, faith, and meaning, and

6. what messages to they tell themselves about the expression or repression of grief as related to their faith.

The Reverend Edgar Jackson[2] wrote the following related to the expression of grief:

> The ability to mourn may not seem to be a major asset in life. Yet as one of the Beatitudes puts it, "Blessed are they that mourn for they shall be comforted." In the Phillips version it reads, "How happy are those who know what sorrow means, for they will be given courage and comfort." A wise nature and spiritual resources together make it possible for us to face the emotional amputation of death and emerge from the experience as wiser and stronger persons. (p. 6)

Your question reminds me of the importance of reminding ourselves that faith does not make one immune from the emotions of grief. Grieving isn't weakness or lack of faith. God does not give out rewards to those who project insulation from the experience of grief. Grief is a friend to be embraced on the journey toward reconciliation. Approaching mourners as a compassionate fellow human being and seeking to understand how their faith impacts on their experience with grief would seem to be much better than either one without the other.

REFERENCES

[1] Sullender, R.S. (1985). *Grief and growth: Pastoral resources for emotional and spiritual growth.* Mahwah, NJ: Paulist Press.

[2] Jackson, E., (1971). *When someone dies.* Philadelphia: Fortress Press.

22
MODEL FOR ASSESSMENT OF THE MOURNER

What suggestions do you have for assessment of the mourner? Are there certain areas that we should be certain to include as we attempt to understand the mourner?

The assessment task is to create an environment that encourages and assists mourners to teach you about their experience with grief; thereby, allowing you to determine how to best assist them in their journey toward reconciliation. Obviously, as continually emphasized in this text, a number of factors will influence the unique journey that each individual mourner experiences. Having a structured assessment framework helps provide for a comprehensive understanding of the mourner.

My preference in providing you some guidelines for assessment is to outline those questions that you as a helper need to ask yourself as you enter the helping relationship with the mourner. Each of us as helpers has our own unique style of gathering the information needed to assist other people. My suggestion is that you work to answer the following questions in the style that is most comfortable for you. Please note that this framework explores the following four areas:

- assessment of those unique factors that serve to influence the mourner's individual response,
- assessment of the mourner's general physical health,
- assessment of the potential of complicated grief responses and common patterns of avoiding grief, and
- assessment of where the mourner is in the process of accomplishing his or her reconciliation needs (tasks of mourning).

1. Assessment of those unique factors that influence the mourner's individual response.

- What was the nature of the relationship that existed between the grieving person and the person that died? What was the nature of the level of attachment in the relationship? What functions did the relationship serve in this person's life?

- Does the person have a positive support system available? Is this support available on an extended basis? Is this person able and willing to accept support from others?

- How has this person responded to prior loss or crises in life? What was this person's personality like prior to the loss, particularly as it relates to self esteem? Does any previous history of mental health related difficulties exist, particularly as relates to depression?

- What was the personality of the person who died like? Based on that person's own unique personality, what role did he or she play within the family, i.e., stabilizer, disrupter, etc.?

- What were the circumstances surrounding the death? How old was the person that died? What is the survivor's perception of the timeliness of the death? Was the death anticipated or was it sudden and unexpected? Does the person have a persistent sense that they should have been able to have prevented the death?

- What is ⸱he survivor's religious and cultural background? How do these backgrounds influence the survivor's ability to give self permission to mourn? What can this person teach me about his or her religious and cultural backgrounds?

- What other stresses does this person have impacting on life at this time? What additional losses have resulted from the death of this person in the mourner's life?

- What is the survivor's previous experiences with death? How have these previous experiences influenced the attitudes and behaviors related to grief?

- How has this person been socially influenced to respond to loss based on the person's sex?

- What was this person's experience with the funeral? Did the funeral experience aid in the expression or repression of the grief? What role does this person believe the funeral played in the experience with grief?

2. Assessment of the mourner's general physical health.

- What is the person's general medical history? What is the current status of the mourner's health?

- What, if any, current medications is the person taking?

- What is this person's drug and alcohol history?

3. Assessment of the potential of complicated grief responses and common patterns of avoiding grief.

- Does the person meet the criteria for any of the four complicated grief responses as outlined in this text:

    a. Absent Grief
    b. Distorted Grief
    c. Converted Grief
    d. Chronic Grief

- Does the person meet the criteria for any of the five common patterns of avoiding grief as outlined in this text:

    a. The Postponer
    b. The Displacer
    c. The Replacer
    d. The Minimizer
    e. The Somaticizer

4. Assessment of where the mourner is in the process of accomplishing his or her reconciliation needs as outlined in this text.

- Where is the person in the process of experiencing and expressing outside of oneself the reality of the death?

- Where is this person in the process of tolerating the emotional suffering inherent in the work of grief while nurturing oneself both physically and emotionally?

- Where is the person in the process of converting the relationship with the deceased from one of presence to a relationship of memory?

- Where is the person in the process of developing a new self-identity based on a life without the deceased?

- Where is the person in the process of relating the experience of loss to a context of meaning?

Responses to these questions evolve over time and should be continually reevaluated in the process of working with the mourner.

23

FUNERAL RITUAL
AND GRIEF

What part does the funeral ritual play in the experience of grief?

As previously noted under factors that influence the mourner's response to death, funerals can potentially assist in social, phychological, and spiritual reconciliation. Historically, evidence has been found that funeral rituals have been used for at least 60,000 years[1]. All forms of ritualization are about the ordering of experience. When a death occurs the funeral ritual provides a structure to assist and support the mourner through the initial period of mourning.

One of the many roles of clergy is to serve as the "coordinator of ritual" that serves to meet the needs of the bereaved. The opportunity to serve as coordinator results in the funeral message and ceremony being a real catalyst that frequently marks the very beginning of the reconciliation process for the mourner. Well-designed funeral rituals carry out the core meaning of the people making use of them, the meanings which often give the mourner the sense that even in death, life goes on.

Perhaps the major role of the funeral is to assist in the "rite of passage"—a phrase coined by Van Gennep[2]. Van Gennep identified the common dynamic operating in various rites which accompany a passage from one social status or group to another, such as rites of birth, marriage, and death. He pointed out that all such rites include three phases: (1) separation from the old status, (2) transition into a new status, and (3) incorporation into that new status. The reconciliation needs (tasks of mourning) outlined in this text are analogous to these rites of passage.

Turner[3] has expanded on these three phases of passage with emphasis on the culture's handling of the second phase of transition into a new status. Turner reminded us that change in an individual's life is a potential threat to the whole social group, which knows how to treat someone who is in a clearly defined state but not someone who hovers between states. This helps explain why many bereaved people are often left feeling abandoned shortly after the funeral. Many people around the mourner feel inadequate in meeting needs during this time of transition, sometimes saying, "I just don't know what to say or do."

DECLINE OF RITUAL

The growing trend toward minimizing the funeral ritual or eliminating it all together has resulted in many people not knowing how to mourn in healthy ways. In eliminating ritual we communicate the need to repress and isolate oneself in the experience of grief. The frequent result is that people grieve in isolation, but do not mourn, i.e., share their grief outside of themselves in a social context.

In comparing modern man to primitive man, Reverend Edgar Jackson[4] wrote the following:

> Because we cannot face our grief in terms of normal expression, we must work out the more costly details of a neurotic grief. Primitive man faced his grief directly and worked out a system of personal and social rituals and symbols that made it possible for him to deal with it directly. Modern man does not seem to know how to proceed in the expression of this fundamental emotion. He has no generally accepted social patterns for dealing with death. His rituals are partial and unsatisfying. His funerals are apt to be meaningless and empty. Either he is so afraid of normal emotion that his funerals are sterile, or they are so steeped in superficialities that they remain meaningless, and the more normal emotions remain unengaged. (pp. 57-58)

Clinical experience suggests that when the funeral ritual is minimized or distorted, that mourning often becomes minimized or distorted. Likewise, when no funeral ritual occurs the mourner often adopts a complicated response style of delayed or absent grief. The growing trend away from traditional forms of funeral ritual puts special emphasis on clergy and other helpers to pastorally and personally attend to the needs of mourners. This special and individualized attention could not be replaced soley by formalized ritual, but the lack of mourning rituals and customs forces the helper to be reminded of the special needs of people who are experiencing grief. And, in the case of clergy, to make mourners a special focus of one's pastoral care.

PURPOSES OF THE FUNERAL

Rando[5] has provided an excellent overview of how funerals benefit the mourner. Rando concentrated on the psychological, social, spiritual and social group benefits to the mourner. Not wishing to outline a topic area that Rando has covered well, the following are those areas she has outlined. For the reader wanting more extensive coverage of these benefits, please see Rando's text.

Psychological Benefits

● Funerals confirm and reinforce the reality of the death.

● Funerals assist in the acknowledgement and expression of feelings of loss.

● Funerals stimulate the recollection of the deceased, a necessary aspect of decathexis.

● Funerals assist mourners in beginning to accommodate to the changed relationship between themselves and the deceased loved one.

● Funerals allow for input from the community that serves as a living memorial to the deceased and helps mourners form an integrated image of the deceased.

● Funerals in and of themselves contain the specific properties of rituals employed in therapy.

Social Benefits

● Funerals allow the community to provide social support to the mourners.

● Funerals provide meaningful, structured activities to counter the loss of predictability and order frequently accompanying the death of a loved one.

● Funerals begin the process of reintegrating the bereaved back into the community.

Spiritual Benefits

- Funerals with a religious orientation give mourners a context of meaning as they attempt to fit the death of their loved one, and ultimately of themselves, into their religious/philosophical framework.

Social Group Benefits

- Funerals help the group to adjust to the loss of one of its members.

- Funerals affirm the social order by offering testimony that despite the death that has occurred, the community lives on.

- Funerals bind the social group together through present experience and collective memory.

- Funerals demonstrate to members of society that they themselves will someday die, and serve as vehicles of anticipartory grief prompted by the rehearsal of their own mortality.

- Funerals are a way in which the community conveys its values and beliefs regarding the meaning of life and death.

- Funerals are means by which the community may maintain symbolic connection with the dead and reap therapeutic opportunities to complete unfinished mourning.

- Funerals provide the final disposition of the body or the remains of the deceased.

We do not need to search through the numerous studies that have been done in recent years to realize that the funeral in contemporary society is many things to many people. We have observed, for example, that the traditional funeral, consisting of a public viewing, a public service, and a public committal service, has been subject to modification and change. New rites for disposition of the dead have emerged. Emergent variability is not only a fact in funeral rituals, but is occurring throughout all of society.

Often in the past people blindly followed tradition in many areas of their lives and in the way they buried their dead. Today, however, we as caregivers are involved with a highly educated public who have been taught to ask the question, "Why?" As a result, we must be prepared not only to answer the "Why?" but to assist in the creation of meaningful funeral services that responds to it.

As previously outlined, two of the major benefits of the funeral are to assist in the acknowledgement and expression of feelings of loss. Among the greatest needs of mourners are to feel and experience the significance of the life the person lived while among them. As a result, a funeral should be a personal celebration both of life and death, of love and hope—these encourage the expression of thoughts and feelings on the part of the bereaved.

We all have observed how the funeral ritual is rich in symbolic forms of expressive communication. Whether it be the music, the setting, the flowers, or the symbols, they all add special significance to the event. The irony of this is that while attempts are made to encourage expression nonverbally, we often discourage any verbal expression on the part of the bereaved. The more emotional stress surrounding a human event, the more most people have difficulty putting their thoughts and feelings into words. They need help! But if they are not offered support and/or choose to eliminate any form of funeral ritual, they will often remain verbally passive and fail to mourn in healthy ways.

Ideally the group setting of the funeral creates an atmosphere whereby it is proper and valid to express emotions. When emotions are repressed or denied, they often find detours that may be a threat to both physical and emotional health. As emphasized throughout this text, if bereaved people are given the opportunity for genuine expression of feelings of grief they are more able to work toward successful reconciliation of the mourning process.

What does all of the previous information tell us about the necessary qualities in persons who have the privilege of conducting funeral rituals? The person who facilitates the funeral must have not only a knowledge of the needs of the bereaved to express authentic feelings, but also must realize the need to affirm finality, the need for meaning, the need for realism, and the need for support. While no two people or no two situations are identical, one can think of needs in general terms as long as enough flexibility is maintained to adapt to individual bereavement.

Those persons who facilitate the funeral must have certain characteristics to enhance effectiveness. They must have an ability to communicate empathy, understanding the situation of the bereaved and knowing something of what they are feeling (see Helping Qualities of the Bereavement Caregiver, pages 159-163). Not attempting to feel their feelings for them, but to give them permission to feel their feelings. Those who facilitate the funeral must be flexible and sensitive, not forcing attitudes or behaviors on mourners that are not genuinely their own.

The importance of the facilitator to establish a personal relationship with the bereaved cannot be overemphasized. The quality of this relationship often becomes a determinant of the degree of helpfulness in the funeral. The facilitator must be able to focus on the individualized needs and feelings of the bereaved. In addition, the facilitator needs an opportunity to meet with the family prior to the funeral, for if he or she does not, the bereaved often will feel distant and depersonalized during the service.

In the final analysis, funeral rituals must be judged on how they help the people involved to fulfill their important emotional needs. Noted author C.S. Lewis has written:

> Those who dislike ritual in general—ritual in any way and every depart-
> ment of life—may be asked most earnestly to reconsider the question. It is a
> pattern imposed on the mere flux of our feelings by reason and will, which
> renders pleasures less fugitive and griefs more endurable, which hands
> over to the power of wise custom the task (to which the individual and his
> moods are so inadequate) of being festive or sober, gay or reverent, when
> we choose to be, and not at the bidding of chance.[6]

REFERENCES

[1] Aries, P. (1981). *The hour of our death.* New York: Alfred A. Knopf.

[2] Van Gennep, A. (1960). *The rites of passage.* Chicago: The University of Chicago.

[3] Turner, V. (1977). *The ritual process.* Ithaca, NY: Cornell University Press.

[4] Jackson, E. (1957). *Understanding grief.* New York: Abingdon.

[5] Rando, T.A. (1984). *Grief, dying, and death: Clinical interventions for care-givers,* Champaign, IL: Research Press.

[6] Lewis, C.S., 1952. *Paradise Lost.* New York: Oxford University Press.

24

CHILDREN AND GRIEF

What role can we as clergy play in helping children with the experience of grief?

Obviously, the clergyperson is often in an excellent position to offer guidance and support to both parents and children during times of death and grief. Clergypersons have the opportunity to provide comprehensive, continuous care to bereaved families while embracing the reality that children are frequently the "forgotten grievers."

We now realize that the capacity to grieve does not focus only on one's abiliity to "understand," but instead upon one's ability to "feel." Any child, regardless of chronological age, that is capable of loving is capable of grieving. While the very young child may not have the ability to comprehend the total meaning of death, primarily because of inability to sense time and space, this inability makes the child's response to acute loss potentially more profound.

Reconciliation to the death of someone loved is typically even more complex for children than for adults. Outward expressions of mourning are not always easily observed in children. Observers expecting to see grief expressed in children in the same way adults mourn may unfortunately assume that children are not influenced by the death. Experience suggests that children ususaly express grief through behavior as opposed to specific words they might say. Careful observations of behavior will provide cues that illustrate the need for ongoing support, understanding, and guidance.

Among other helping roles, clergypersons can

1. encourage families to include children in the events surrounding death;

2. educate parents regarding typical ways in which children express grief;

3. create an open atmosphere that encourages children to ask questions about death, dying, and grief;

4. develop a caregiving relationship with children that informs them of the clergyperson's individual emotional availability to them; and

5. model for children the reality that grief is a privilege that results from the capacity to give and receive love.

Experiences with loss and grief are an integral part of the natural development and growth of the child and the family. The clergyperson's willingness and capacity to "be with" the family during times of grief can be difficult, time-consuming, and emotionally draining, however, this time also can be among the most rewarding of caregiving opportunities.

Are there certain age-level classifications of children's capacity to understand death?

Like all areas of development, children's capacity to understand death, grow and expands as children mature. To this date, in a number of studies tremendous variability has been found regarding the specific age at which a mature understanding of death is achieved.[1] [2] [3] This variability appears to be affected by personality factors, sociocultural factors, nature of the death, and probably a multitude of other factors that are unidentified at this time. As a result, caregivers must keep in mind that each child is a individual shaped by experiences of life.

For our current purposes, let us recognize that a number of investigators have attempted to outline various age-level classifications at which specific ideas related to death occur. Outcomes from the investigations lack total agreement on specifics associated with death as determined by the age of the child. However, all investigators do agree that associations move from no understanding toward specifics which is a developmental concept. Therefore, chronological age is one way of making some attempt to classify what might be expected in terms of understanding death.

In summary, children do appear to proceed from little or no understanding of death to recognition of the concept in realistic form. While most often levels of understanding are listed in chronological order, the individual child may well deviate from the specific age range and particular behavior associated with that age. All of us as careproviders have had the experience of working with some eight-year-olds who are more mature than other sixteen-year-olds with whom we have worked.

While evidence does appear for the age-level understanding of children's concepts of death, one needs to keep in mind that development involves much more than simply growing older. Environmental support, behavior, attitudes, responsiveness of adults, self-concept, intelligence, previous experiences with death, and a number of other factors have an important role in the individual child's understanding of death.

What emotional responses might we witness in the bereaved child?

To provide an adequate response to this question would require that I go beyond the scope of this text. However, for a detailed review of this author's perceptions of children's emotional responses to death, the reader is referred to my text, *Helping Children Cope With Grief*[4]. In Figure 8 is provided a brief outline of typical responses caregivers are likely to observe in children who are mourning.

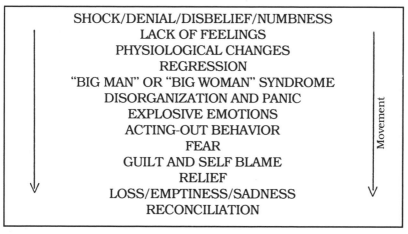

SHOCK/DENIAL/DISBELIEF/NUMBNESS
LACK OF FEELINGS
PHYSIOLOGICAL CHANGES
REGRESSION
"BIG MAN" OR "BIG WOMAN" SYNDROME
DISORGANIZATION AND PANIC
EXPLOSIVE EMOTIONS
ACTING-OUT BEHAVIOR
FEAR
GUILT AND SELF BLAME
RELIEF
LOSS/EMPTINESS/SADNESS
RECONCILIATION

Movement

Figure 8. Dimensions of Childhood Grief

Should children be allowed to attend the funeral?

Experience suggests that the funeral is a significant occasion in the life of the entire family. Since the funeral is a significant event, children should have the same opportunity to attend as any other member of the family.

Yes, children should be "allowed" to attend, but never forced. Children can often sense whether adults around them will be able to make the experience a meaningful and comfortable experience and on that basis make a decision to attend or not attend. By encouraging children to be a part of the group sharing of a common loss, we as adults help them acknowledge the reality and finality of death.

An area of discussion that clergypersons can help remind parents to talk about with children is the "why" of going to the funeral. Adults sometimes talk about going to funerals, but fail to talk about why they are going. Encourage parents to explain the purpose of a funeral: as a time to honor the person who has died, as a time to help, comfort, and support each other; and as a time to affirm that life continues.

Children's first visit to a funeral home is often best experienced with only a few people who are especially close. This allows children to react and express feelings freely and to talk about any concerns they might have. Children should be encouraged to ask questions and provided opportunities to do so prior to, during, and after the funeral.

Viewing the body of someone loved also can be a positive experience. Adult's would do well to remember that children have no innate fears about the dead body. Seeing the body provides an opportunity to say "goodbye" and helps prevent fears that are often much worse than reality. As with attending the funeral, however, seeing the body should not be forced. While children, particularly young children, may not completely understand the ceremony surrounding death, being involved in the funeral helps establish a sense of comfort and the understanding that life goes on even though someone loved has died.

What about sharing religious beliefs about death with children?

By the very nature of being a clergyperson you will be called upon to teach the religious beliefs of your denomination as related to life and death. While no simple guidelines exist that make this an easy task, the key, as with most experiences in life, appears to be honesty.

Adults can only share with children those concepts they truly believe. You can help parents understand that children need not understand and grasp the total religious philosophy of the adult world. Any religious explanations about death are best described in concrete, practical terms; children have difficulty understanding abstractions. The theological correctness of the information is less important at this time than the fact the adult is communicating in a loving way. Help parents understand that one need not feel guilty or ashamed if "God" and "Heaven" cannot be explained with exact definitions. Many occurrences in life can be enriched by approaching them with mystery and awe.

How important are other family members regarding children's ability to mourn?

Experience suggests that the significant adults in children's lives are the most important factor in allowing and encouraging children to mourn. Children's ability to share their grief outside of themselves depends on the capacity of significant adults' expressing their own grief and conveying to children that they too can express a full spectrum of feelings. The sharing of grief between parents and children assists the family in recognizing both the uniqueness and commonality of their experience. This means that the children can learn that mom and dad will be sad at times, but that this feeling is normal and not a rejection of the children.

When children experience those times in life when their parents are sad, or hurt, or lonely, or whatever the feeling may be, and also realize that as children they are not responsible for these feelings, the result is that children learn to express freely their own wide range of feelings following loss. Clergyperson's are often a vital link in helping families understand the importance of modeling the open expression of feelings. As emphasized as a theme throughout this text—pain is healed through the outward expression of mourning. Should significant adults surrounding children fail to share their own loss related thoughts and feelings, chances are that the children all grieve in isolation while failing to mourn outside of themselves.

Could you explain your use of the term "open-system family" as it relates to children and expression of mourning?

In referring to the "open-system family" I mean those families that permit and encourage the open and honest self-expression of its members. In such a family children are accepted as integral parts of the family and capable of understanding at their own level of development. Children are not seen as little and as a result bad. In such a family, differences in terms of the meaning of the death are viewed as natural and are able to be discussed. In an "open-system family" children can participate in decision making; accept any and all feelings of grief; and say what they think and feel in that grief is viewed as an opportunity for growth.

Conversely in a "closed-system family" children are often encouraged to repress, deny, and hide their grief. The primary rule is that everyone in the family is supposed to think and feel the same way and as a result no need exists to talk about thoughts and feelings. In such a family, expression of grief is often impossible, and if it does occur, the expression is viewed as being abnormal or "sick." Children in this kind of family often carry their grief around with them for years and express it in various sorts of emotional and behavioral disturbances.

In summary, caring adults need to communicate to children that feelings of grief are not something to be ashamed of or something to hide. Instead, grief is a natural expression of love for the person who died.

As caring adults, the challenge is clear: children do not choose between grieving and not grieving; adults, one the other hand, do have a choice—to help or not to help children cope with grief. With love, understanding, and knowledge of helping skills, we as adult caregivers can guide children through this vulnerable time and help make the experience a valuable part of children's personal growth and development.

REFERENCES

[1] Nagy, M. (1948). The child's theories concerning death. *Journal of Genetic Psychology, 73:* 3-27.

[2] Anthony, S. (1971). *The discovery of death in childhood and after.* London: Allan Lan, Penquin.

[3] Furman, E. (1974). *A child's parent dies.* New Haven: Yale University Press.

[4] Wolfelt, A. (1983). *Helping children cope with grief.* Muncie, IN: Accelerated Development, Publishers.

NOTES

25

HELPING QUALITIES OF THE BEREAVEMENT CAREGIVER

What helping qualities can I as a clergyperson bring to bereaved persons that will encourage them to share their experience of grief with me?

This question provides us with an opportunity to outline those personal qualities of helpers that serve to form the foundation of a supportive relationship with the bereaved person. In a sense, we are asking, "How can we establish a relationship with the mourner that provides a safe environment wherein he or she feels free to express grief without fear of judgement, isolation, or abandonment?" While impossible through one's pastoral presence to do away with the work of grief that must be done, what is possible is to make more tolerable the sense of aloneness that most mourners experience. What follows is an outline of several of the qualities that help create conditions for healing in the bereaved. These helping qualities are not intended to be all inclusive.

EMPATHY

Perhaps the most complex, vital, and fundamental quality for caregivers of the bereaved is the ability to convey accurate empathy. Empathetic responsiveness requires the ability to go beyond the surface and to become involved in the mourner's feeling world, but always with the "as if" quality of taking another's role without personally experiencing what the other person experiences. If you experienced the same emotions as the person you were trying to help, you would be over involved. Obviously, unless you have experienced the same type of loss as the person you are attempting to help, your empathy will naturally be incomplete.

If you think you will be unaffected by empathizing with bereaved people, you are only fooling yourself. If you work to empathize with the mourner you will open yourself to the intense pain, fear, and deep sadness that is shared with you. The ability to empathize means a willingness to be involved in the emotional suffering that is inherent in the work of grief.

Empathizing with the mourner also requires the willingness to tolerate primitive needs for dependency that commonly evolve in the mourner. If you as a helper become frightened by this temporary dependence, chances are you will communicate a rejection of the mourner; the very thing they often fear the most.

To have empathy for the mourner does not constitute the direct expression of one's own feelings, but rather focuses exclusively on the feelings expressed by another, and thereby conveying an understanding of them. In other words, empathetic communication with the mourner means to strive to understand the meaning of his or her experience rather than imposing meaning on that experience from the outside.

Empathy is communicated when the mourner feels you "understand." As you know, to say simply, "I understand how you feel" is not enough. Empathy is communicated when you respond at the emotional, feeling level of the mourner. You reach the mourner where he or she is right now, and the result is a feeling of being understood and supported.

Related to the communication of empathy, I find that many caregivers new to bereavement care hesitate to elicit and embrace in the mourner such feelings as despair, sadness, loneliness, and hurt, often fearing that expression and exploration of these feelings will only "make matters worse." However, experience suggests that such hesitation is a form of defensive protection for the helper who finds it threatening to respond at any true emotional level to the mourner. While some forms of complicated grief require movement away from eliciting mourners' deep feelings (example: chronic grief), normal grief must be expressed for healing to occur. Just because feelings are threatening does not mean that we as helpers should avoid encouraging their expression in the mourner. Gendlin[1] has written about the expression of feeling by noting, "We should never avoid what an individual implicity feels because we fear he cannot take it. He is already taking it! The question is: "Will you enable him to live it with you or only alone?"' (p.91). For our purposes, we might also alter Gendlin's observation to read as follows: "We should never avoid what a mourner implicitly feels because we fear **we** cannot take it."

The communication of accurate empathy has a number of benefits for the mourner. Among them are the following:

1. Empathetic communication is a foundation upon which you establish a helping relationship with the mourner.

2. The mourner who feels empathetically understood is more likely to risk sharing deep and personal feelings.

3. The mourner's experience of your genuine effort and commitment to understand creates a trusting, low threat environment that negates the need for self-protection and isolation.

4. The communication of empathy encourages self-exploration in the mourner, a prerequisite for self-understanding and eventual movement toward reconciliation.

5. Empathetic communication creates conditions that allow for the clarification of thoughts and feelings in the mourner, many of which were previously puzzling in the person.

RESPECT

In the context of helping the mourner, respect refers to a nonpossessive caring for and affirmation of the person as a separate individual capable of reaching reconciliation in his or her grief. This quality involves a receptive attitude of having the mourner "teach you" about his or her experience with grief. This means that even the mourner's defenses and normal resistances to do the work of mourning are met with patience and a desire to understand the function they are serving for him or her. Respect is an attitude of trying to never purposely damage or hurt a mourner's self-esteem.

Respecting the mourner includes an effort to create a cooperative helping partnership in which what is created is a sense of working together toward mutual goals of healing grief's hurts. The opposite of this respectful cooperative partnership would be the helper who presumptuously believes that his or her superior knowledge of grief qualifies him or her to project what is best for the mourner to think, feel, and do.

WARMTH AND CARING

Warmth and caring in the helper is demonstrated through a sense of personal closeness to the mourner as opposed to professional distance. Showing you are warm and caring is particularly helpful in the early phases of building a relationship with the mourner.

The quality of warmth is communicated primarily nonverbally to the mourner. For example, showing supportive concern through facial gestures and touch are two important ways of communicating warmth and caring. As the saying goes, "People don't care how much you know until they know how much you care". This is very true with people in acute grief who are extremely sensitive to who understands and cares and who does not.

SELF-AWARENESS

Caregivers who continually work to develop an understanding of their own experiences with loss are more likely to be effective helpers to the bereaved. Helpers who are self-aware continually ask themselves questions like, "How am I being impacted by sharing in the mourners experience with grief?" "Does the mourner's experience with loss remind me of some of my own losses?", "Where can I share the feelings that supporting this mourner stimulate in me?" Self-awareness also means that the helper is open to learning what each new counseling relationship with mourners has to teach the caregiver about being helpful at this time.

CONGRUENCE

Congruence in working with bereaved persons means the caregiver models those beliefs about mourning that he or she embraces as being important to the bereaved. For example, if the caregiver believes to express feelings after experiencing loss is important, he or she would not try to hide these feelings from people around him or her. To do otherwise would be to project that "it is o.k. for others to grieve, but I don't need to do so." For clergy (excuse the pun), this means practicing what one preaches.

KNOWLEDGE

Knowledge means that caregivers are aware of the body of knowledge available related to the experience of mourning. Knowledge of applied research findings and a sound theoretical understanding of grief helps put care into action. For example, experience combined with knowledge assists the caregiver in knowing when to shift away from encouraging the expression of feelings and toward the need to discourage emotionality.

The six qualities described combine to create a healing environment that allows for the acceptance and sharing of grief. Perhaps beyond these qualities is an attitude-an attitude that grief is not an enemy to overcome, but a privilege to be experienced as a result of having loved.

REFERENCES

[1] Gendlin, E.T. (1970). Existentialism and experiential psychotherapy. In J.T. Hart & T.M. Tomlinson (Eds.), *New direction in client-centered therapy.* Boston: Houghton Mifflin.

NOTES

26

HELPING TASKS OF THE CAREGIVER

You have outlined what you termed "reconciliation needs" or tasks of mourning for the bereaved person. What about tasks or principles of helping for the caregiver to keep in mind?

Several authors have outlined what could be termed tasks for caregivers of the bereaved. In an outline format this section will review different guidelines that have been proposed as procedures or tasks for caregivers of the bereaved to consider. For more detailed information the reader is referred to the original references found at the conclusion of this section. In addition, you will find this author's own general outline of helping tasks for caregivers of the bereaved.

Corazzini[1] has outlined four major tasks of the caregiver:

1. Remaining open to the loss of the other and resisting blocking or discounting the process.

2. Develop empathy with the bereaved which permits the counselor to experience the complex feelings of the bereaved and to communicate understanding of the experience to the bereaved person.

3. Encouraging reminiscing, which seems essential to moving through the grief process.

4. Insisting on the loss by reminding the mourner that death has really occurred, especially in the first few days of bereavement.

Raphael[2] also has outlined four major tasks of the caregiver:

1. To offer basic human comfort and support.

2. To encourage the expression of grief.

3. To promote the mourning process.

4. To supplement the personal support system which already exists in order to facilitate the process of grief.

Worden[3] has outlined ten major tasks for the caregiver:

1. Help the survivor actualize the loss.

2. Help the survivor to identify and express feelings.

3. Assist living without the deceased.

4. Facilitate emotional withdrawal from the deceased.

5. Provide time to grieve.

6. Interpret "normal" behavior.

7. Allow for individual differences.

8. Provide continuing support.

9. Examine defenses and coping styles.

10. Identify pathology and refer.

Rando[4] has provided an excellent comprehensive outline that she has grouped into seven broad phases:

1. Make contact and assess

- Reach out to the bereaved.
- Be present physically, as well as emotionally, to render the griever security and support.

- Make sure you give the person "permission" to grieve.
- Do not allow the griever to remain isolated.
- Maintain a family systems perspective in dealing with the griever.
- Conduct an assessment of the mourner's grief.
- Assess to determine which tasks of grief are incomplete.
- Make sure that the griever has appropriate medical evaluation and treatment when symptoms warrant.

2. Maintain a therapeutic and realistic perspective

- Remember that you cannot take away the pain from the bereaved.
- Do not let your own sense of helplessness keep you from reaching out to the griever.
- Expect to have to tolerate volatile reactions from the bereaved.
- Recognize the critical therapeutic value of "the gift of presence."
- Make sure you view the loss from the griever's unique perspective.
- Let your genuine concern and caring show.
- Do not let your own needs determine the experience for the griever.
- Do not try to explain the death in religious or philosophical terms too early.
- Do not tell the griever to feel better because there are other loved ones who are still alive.
- Do not try to unrealistically "pretty up" the situation.
- Do not forget to plant the seeds of hope.
- Do not encourage responses antithetical to appropriate grief.
- Maintain an appropriate distance from the griever.
- Do not fail to hold out the expectation that the griever will successfully complete the tasks of mourning and that the pain will subside.

3. Encourage verbalization of feelings and recollection of the deceased

- Help the bereaved to recognize, actualize, and accept the loss.
- Listen nonjudgmentally and with permissiveness and acceptance.
- Assist the griever in identifying, accepting, and expressing all the various feelings of grief.
- If the griever appears to be resisting the grief process, explore the griever's defenses to discover the reasons behind it.
- Allow the bereaved to cry and cry, talk and talk, review and review without the interruption of your sanity.
- Do not be amazed if the griever talks about many of the same things repeatedly.
- Do not be afraid to mention the dead person to the griever.
- Encourage the griever to realistically review and talk about the deceased and their mutual relationship.

4. Help the griever identify and resolve secondary losses and unfinished business

- Help the griever to identify current and potential secondary losses (physical and symbolic) resulting from the death.
- Help the griever to identify any unfinished business with the deceased and look for appropriate ways to facilitate closure.
- Assist the griever in recognizing that not only must she grieve for the deceased individual, but also for the dreams, fantasies, and expectations that she had for and with the deceased.

5. Support the griever in coping with the grief process

- Design interventions that capitalize upon the griever's positive coping skills and compensate for deficient ones.

- Provide the griever with formative data about the grief process.
- Make sure the griever understands that her grief reactions will be unique.
- Communicate your realistic understanding of the pain and the griever's natural wish to avoid it.
- Help the griever to recognize that she must yield to the painful process of grief.
- Make it clear to the griever that the process of grief will affect all areas of her life.
- Assist the griever with appropriate time and course expectations.
- Encourage the griever to be patient and not to expect too much of herself.
- Help the griever find a variety of ways to replenish herself following the severe depletion resulting from major loss.
- Suggest some form of physical activity to release pent-up feelings.
- Help the griever maintain good physical health.
- Do not support flight by the bereaved.
- Help the bereaved to deal with practical problems that develop as a consequence of the death.

6. Help the griever to accommodate to the loss

- Assist the bereaved in getting and maintaining the proper perspective on what resolution of grief will mean.
- Help the griever recognize that a major loss always changes us to some extent.
- Help the bereaved to discover his new identity and the psychological and social role that he must assume or relinquish as a consequence of the death.
- Assess with the griever which roles and skills must be assumed and work to help him accomplish this.
- Help the griever to understand that a healthy new relationship with the deceased must be formed.
- Ask the griever in what appropriate ways he will keep the deceased's memory alive and continue to relate to her.

- Do not allow the griever to equate the length and amount of his suffering with some kind of testimony to his love for the deceased.
- Assist the griever in reestablishing a system of belief of meaning.

7. Work with the griever to reinvest in a new life

- At the appropriate time, encourage the griever to find rewarding new things to do and people to invest in.
- Do not push the bereaved into new relationships before they are ready.
- Help the griever identify the gain that has derived from the loss.

A brief outline of this author's perception of seven major tasks of the caregiver is as follows:

1. Listening to the bereaved

   As described under qualities of the caregiver (see pages 159-163), empathetic listening is an essential helping principle. To listen effectively means that the caregiver does not have all of the answers and needs the communication of the mourner as a guide to know how to respond in helpful ways. The mourner feels validated when he or she is heard. Empathic listening allows the caregiver to "be with" the mourner encouraging the expression of grief and the telling of one's story.

2. Understanding the bereaved

   To understand the bereaved means to be familiar with those thoughts, feelings and behaviors common to the experience of grief. Beyond understanding is the task of communicating this understanding back to the bereaved in a helpful way. This capacity to understand is achieved by caregivers who adopt an orientation of "teach me" about your experience of grief. Then, as the teaching-learning process evolves, genuine attempts are made to communicate in harmony with the mourner.

3. Educating the bereaved

A critical helping task for the caregiver is to help normalize the bereaved person's experience with grief. Many newly bereaved persons are not familiar with what is normal in grief, particularly when they have no prior experience with loss in their lives. An important procedure is to help mourners know that they are not "going crazy" as they begin the journey through grief. Knowledge about the experience of bereavement usually encourages the expression of thoughts and feelings of grief. For example, knowledge that pain is something to be expected often allows the mourner to enter more fully into the experience as opposed to working consciously or unconsciously to avoid the experience.

4. Supporting the bereaved

The process of supporting the bereaved follows naturally from educating. To support means to accompany mourners on the journey through the healthy reconciliation of grief. The caregiver's supportive counseling skills provide structure and validation for the expression of grief. Borrowing a sense of support from outside of themselves allows mourners to survive the pain of the loss.

The caregiver needs to be capable of enduring the intensity of the grief and willing to "be with" mourners as they confront the depth of their loss. To support also means the caregiver gives mourners permission to be temporarily dependent on others, while realizing that this dependence is not permanent or pathological.

5. Advocating for the bereaved

The caregiver will at times need to advocate for bereaved persons. For example, the caregiver may need to provide direct intervention ("intervention" literally means "coming between" someone and their problems) to assist in providing for some time off work after a death. Advocating for the bereaved might also involve providing trusted resources to assist the mourner with financial planning, obtaining social security or veterans' benefits, or assistance with legal matters. In addition, advocating for the bereaved is to provide for a safe place where persons can come and not be judged, but accepted for where they are in the experience of grief.

6. Encouraging the bereaved

Encouraging the bereaved relates to movement toward reconciliation. Encouraging means a belief and an attitude that projects a hopefulness about the mourner's capacity to achieve reconciliation. Encouraging is a process of assisting mourners in restoring a sense of self, establishing new relationships and activities, and to go on living while at the same time acknowledging that a significant loss has occurred. In addition, encouraging means to accompany mourners on the experience of relating their loss to a context of meaning.

7. Referring the bereaved

Referring the bereaved is a necessary skill for all caregivers, including clergy. Appropriate referral means the caregiver must be aware of his or her own level of counseling skills related to bereavement care, and when necessary skillfully facilitate the transfer of care to a qualified helper. Some complicated grief responses require specialized interventions and additional training. The skillful facilitation of referral is an art that must be practiced over time. If mourners' feel "dumped" by caregivers, their journey through grief can become further complicated. For additional information on the art of referral, see Lee's[5] article on "Referral as an Act of Pastoral Care."

Obviously, the preceding outline of tasks of the caregiver are only intended as general guidelines. No substitute can be given for formalized training, supervised rehearsal, and real life counseling experience with bereaved persons.

REFERENCES

1 Corazzini, J.G. (1980). The theory and practice of loss therapy. In B.M. Schoenberg (Ed.), *Bereavement counseling: A multi-disciplinary handbook.* Westport, CT: Greenwood.

2 Raphael, B. (1980). A psychiatric model for bereavement counseling. In B.M. Schoenberg (Ed.), *Bereavement counseling: A multi-disciplinary handbook.* Westport, CT: Greenwood.

3 Worden, J.W. (1982). *Grief counseling and grief therapy: A handbook for the mental health practitioner.* New York: Springer.

4 Rando, T.A. (1984). *Grief, dying, and death: Clinical interventions for caregivers.* Champaign, IL: Research Press.

5 Lee, R.R. (1976). Referral as an act of pastoral care. *Journal of Pastoral Care, 30,* 3, 186-197.

NOTES

27

CARING FOR
THE CAREGIVER

What thoughts do you have on caring for oneself as a caregiver in the area of bereavement counseling?

As stated in the Preface to this text, few helping situations are more challenging, nor more rewarding, than the opportunity to assist persons impacted by loss in their lives. Obviously no caregiver to the bereaved can avoid the special stress that comes with entering into the helping relationship. Assisting mourners is a demanding interpersonal process that requires energy and focus. Caregivers who work with people experiencing grief must confront their own losses, fears, hopes, and dreams surrounding both life and death.

Whenever we attempt to respond to the needs of people in grief, the chances are slim that we can, or should, avoid the stress of emotional involvement. The key is what we choose to do with the stress. As you work with people in grief you open yourself to care about them and their movement toward reconciliation. Genuinely caring about the mourner and sharing with him or her some of the most difficult of times in life, eventually touches the depths of your own heart and soul.

Sometimes, caregivers of the bereaved discover churned up feelings related to influences such as bereavement overload, unrealistic expectations about helping all the grief-stricken people in one's community, or perhaps discovering that, at times, one cares more about the mourner's healing process than the person seem to care. The result of these influences is potentially what we might term "bereavement caregiver burn-out." Symptoms of this burn-out syndrome include the following:

1. exhaustion and loss of energy,
2. irritability and impatience,

3. cynicism and detachment,
4. physical complaints and depression,
5. disorganization and confusion,
6. omnipotence and feeling indispensable, and
7. minimization and denial of feelings.

EXHAUSTION AND LOSS OF ENERGY

Feelings of exhaustion and loss of energy are usually among the first signals of caregiver distress. Low energy for the clergyperson, or other caregiver, is often difficult to acknowledge because this is opposite of the high energy level required to meet demands that are both self-imposed and experienced from the outside.

IRRITABILITY AND IMPATIENCE

As stress builds from within irritability and impatience become an inherent component of the experience of burn-out. As caregivers we have typically been used to experiencing a sense of accomplishment and reward for our efforts. As stress increases the ability to feel reward diminishes while our irritability and impatience becomes heightened. Disagreements and tendencies to blame others for any interpersonal difficulties occur as stress takes it's toll on our sense of emotional and physical well-being.

CYNICISM AND DETACHMENT

As caregivers, experiencing emotional burn-out, we may begin to respond to stress in a manner that saves something of ourselves. We may begin to question the value of helping the bereaved, of our family life, of friendships, even of life itself. We may become skeptical of the mourners desire to help oneself heal and work to create distance between ourselves and the person. We may work to convince ourselves, "There is no point in getting involved" as we rationalize our need to distance ourselves from the stress of interpersonal encounter. Detachment serves to help distance ourselves from feelings of pain, helplessness, and hurt.

PHYSICAL COMPLAINTS AND DEPRESSION

Physical complaints, real or imagined, are often induced in bereavement caregivers suffering from burn-out. Often, physical complaints are easier for us to talk about than emotional complaints. The process of consciously or unconsciously converting emotional conflicts may result in a variety of somatic symptoms like headaches, stomachaches, backaches, and long-lasting colds. These symptoms are cues related to the potential of stress overload.

Generalized feelings of depression also are common to the phenomenon of bereavement caregiver burn-out. Loss of appetite, difficulty sleeping, sudden changes in mood, and lethargy suggest that depression has become a part of the overall stress syndrome. Depression is a constellation of symptoms that tell us something is wrong to which we need to pay attention and work to understand.

DISORIENTATION AND CONFUSION

Feelings of disorientation and confusion are often experienced as a component of burn-out. As our minds shift from one topic to another, focusing on current tasks becomes difficult. We may feel busy, yet not accomplish much at all. Since difficulty focusing results in a lack of personal sense of competence, confusion only results in more heightened feelings of disorientation. Thus, a cycle of confusion resulting in more disorientation evolves and becomes difficult to break. The ability to think clearly suffers and concentration and memory are impaired. In addition, the ability to make decisions and sound judgements becomes limited. Obviously our system is overloaded and in need of a break from the continuing cycle of stress.

OMNIPOTENCE AND FEELING INDISPENSIBLE

Another common symptom of bereavement caregiver burn-out is a sense of omnipotence and feeling indispensable. Statements like, "No one else can provide the kind of grief counseling that I can. I have got to be the one to help these people in grief" is not simply the expression of a normal ego. Other persons can provide sound grief counseling and many do it very well. If we as caregivers begin to feel indispensable, we typically block our own as well as others growth. Thinking that no one else can provide adequate counsel but ourself is an obvious indication of stress overload.

MINIMIZATION AND DENIAL OF FEELINGS

Some caregivers when stressed to their limits continue to minimize, if not deny, feelings of burn-out. The caregiver who minimizes is aware of feeling stressed, but when felt, works to minimize the feelings by diluting them through a variety of rationalizations. From a self-perspective minimizing stress seems to work, particularly because it is commensurate with the self-imposed helping principle of "being all things to all people." However, internally repressed feelings of stress build within and emotional strain results.

Perhaps the most dangerous characteristic of the bereavement caregiver burn-out syndrome is the total denial of feelings of stress. As denial takes over, the caregiver's symptoms of stress become enemies to be fought instead of friends to be understood. Regardless of how loud the mind and body cry out for relief, no one is listening.

The specific reasons caregivers adopt denial of feelings of stress are often multiple and complex. For our purposes here we will note that when we care deeply for people in grief we open ourselves to our own vulnerabilities related to loss issues. Perhaps another person's grief stimulates memories of some old griefs of our own. Perhaps those we wish to help frustrate our efforts to be supportive and offer guidance. Whatever the reason the natural way to prevent ourselves from being hurt or disappointed is to deny feelings in general. This denial of feelings is often accompanied by an internal sense of a lack of purpose in what you are doing, in that the willingness and ability to feel are ultimately what gives meaning to life.

This list of symptoms is not intended to be all-inclusive and the various symptoms previously described are not mutually exclusive. The majority of over-stressed caregivers will experience a combination of symptoms. The specific combination of symptoms will vary dependent on such influences as basic personality and the person's caregiving history.

Of all of the stresses inherent in caregivers to the bereaved, emotional involvements appear central to the potential of suffering from burn-out. Perhaps we should ask ourselves what we lose when we decide to minimize or ignore the significant level of emotional involvement that occurs in caring for the bereaved? We probably will discover that in the process of minimizing or ignoring we are, in fact, eliminating our potential to help of its most important component—the all powerful reality that caring about people in grief while at the same time *caring for oneself* is vital to helping people move toward reconciliation.

As caregivers to the bereaved we probably need to remind ourselves that we are our own most important counseling instrument and that what we know about ourselves makes a tremendous difference in our capacity to assist mourners. While the admirable goal of helping others may seem to justify emotional sacrifices, ultimately we are not helping others effectively when we ignore what we are experiencing within ourselves.

If we are to achieve successfully the ability to care for ourselves as caregivers, we must focus on ourselves. We begin to manage the stress inherent in helping the bereaved when we work to understand the defenses we use in the context of our helping tasks. If we acknowledge that effective interpersonal helping always tied to the relationship we establish with the mourner, then we must focus on ourselves as we are involved with that person. Sometimes we think that our helping task is the opposite—that in gathering as much information and knowledge about those we are attempting to assist that we are doing a good job. While we would be remiss to negate the importance of working to understand those we are helping, we would be totally remiss if we did not take ourselves and how we are impacted by involvement in the helping relationship into account. This relates to the demanding dual focus that is essential to being an effective helper to the bereaved.

Experience suggests that practice is needed to work toward an understanding of what is taking place inside ourself, while trying to grasp what is taking place inside others. After all, these thoughts and feelings occur simultaneously; they are usually significantly interrelated. Obviously, you cannot draw close to others without beginning to affect and be affected by them. This is the nature of helping relationships with the bereaved. You cannot help others from a protective position. Helping occurs openly where you are defenseless—if you allow yourself to be. Again, this double focus on the mourner and on yourself is essential to the task of being an effective helper.

As caregivers to the bereaved, an important recognition is that on occasions we too need a supportive relationship where we can be listened to and accepted-to recharge our emotional batteries. Few people who have ever tried to respond to the needs of others in a helping relationship have escaped the stress that comes from emotional involvement. Involving yourself with others, particularly at a time of death and grief, requires taking care of oneself as well as others. Emotional overload, circumstances surrounding deaths and caring about people will ultimately result in times of inevitable stress. When this occurs, we should feel no sense of inadequacy or stigma if we also need the support and understanding of a caring relationship.

28

A FINAL WORD

The opportunity to assist people in grief is a privilege that requires advanced counseling skills combined with compassionate and effective experience in interpersonal involvement. Again, my hope is that this book will help you as a clergyperson use the capacity of your own understanding in a measured, yet powerfully effective way.

To experience and embrace the pain of loss is just as much a part of life as to experience the joy of love. As it should be, thoughts, feelings, and behaviors, that result from the death of a person who has been loved are impossible to ignore. The experience of grief is very powerful. As we encounter personal loss in our lives, we have the opportunity to make a willful choice of how we are going to use the pain of the grief-whether we are going to channel it to make our lives better or worse.

Just as we are faced with choices in our personal experience with loss, we also are faced with choices in our life's work as caregivers. We can choose to help people avoid the work of their grief by encouraging them to repress or deny the wounds of grief, or, we can support and accompany people as they fully enter into their grief. If we are able to achieve the latter of these choices, chances are we can become a catalyst for a renewed sense of meaning and purpose in the lives of our fellow human beings.

NOTES

SUPPORT GROUPS AND ORGANIZATIONS

As clergy, you are frequently called upon to make referrals to local, regional, and national support groups and organizations. The following is a list of some groups and organizations that will help you locate supportive resources for those persons who seek your assistance.

American Association for Marriage and Family Therapy
1717 K Street, N.W.
Suite 407
Washington, DC 20006

> An association of persons who specializes in all phases of marriage and family life. Members include persons trained in pastoral counseling, marriage and family therapy; psychology, psychiatry, and social work.

Amend
4324 Berrywick Terrace
St. Louis, MO 63128

> An international organization of parents of children who have had or do have cancer. Available to offer support and guidance to other parents.

Association for Death Education and Counseling
2211 Arthur Avenue
Lakewood, OH 44107

> This organization is comprised of professionals and lay persons whose goals center around the promotion of death education, death-related counseling, and grief management in education institutions, residential facilities, churches, community and non-profit organizations and related settings.

The Compassionate Friends
P.O. Box 1347
Oak Brook, IL 60521

A self-help organization of bereaved parents. Also has publications available on a wide variety of topics.

Center For Death Education and Research
1167 Social Science Building
University of Minnesota
Minneapolis, MN 55455

A research and information center. Numerous professional and nontechnical publications are available, as well as audiovisual resources.

Center For Loss and Life Transition
3735 Broken Bow Road
Fort Collins, CO 80526

An organization specializing in bereavement education, training, and clinical care. A special focus is on workshop presentations to both professional and lay audiences throughout the country. A variety of educational materials in the area of death and grief are available upon request.

Family Services America
11700 West Lake Park Drive
Park Place
Milwaukee, WI 53224

An organization that helps families under stress. Provides family counseling services and education resources.

Foundation of Thanatology
630 West 168th Street
New York, NY 10032

Sponsors conferences and publishes materials focusing on death, dying, and bereavement.

International Order of The Golden Rule
1000 Churchhill Road
Springfield, IL 62702

Provides educational materials concerning funerals, as well as death, dying, and bereavement.

National Council of Family Relations
1219 University Avenue, S.E.
Minnepolis, MN 55415

An educational and referral source for families under stress.

National Funeral Directors Association
11121 West Oklahoma Avenue
Milwaukee, WI 53227

Provides educational materials concerning funerals, as well as death, dying, and bereavement.

National Hospice Organization
1901 N. Fort Myers Drive
Suite 307
Arlington, VA 22209

Community-based organizations of volunteers, lay persons, and professionals who have received training in palliative care for dying persons. Many also have support services available after death.

National Sudden Infant Death Syndrome Foundation
2 Metro Plaza, Suite 205
8320 Professional Place
Landover, MD 20785

A national organization consisting of chapters for parents who have experienced the death of a child to SIDS. Educational materials are also available.

Parents Without Partners
7910 Woodmont Avenue
Suite 1008
Bethesda, MD 20814

An organization of single parents and their children. Educational and discussion groups are held.

The Samaritans
500 Commonwealth Avenue
Boston, MA 02215

A group of volunteers trained to respond to persons considering suicide or persons who have experienced the death of a friend or relative to suicide.

The Self-Help Center
1600 Dodge Avenue, Suite S-122
Evanston, IL 60204

This organization is a clearing house for self-help groups. This resource can provide referrals to different groups throughout the country.

The Theos Foundation
Clark Building, Suite 1301
717 Liberty Avenue
Pittsburgh, PA 15222

This is a national self-help organization that has groups available to assist young and middle-aged widowed persons. Educational materials also are available.

The Widowed Persons Service
1909 K Street, N.W., Room 580
Washington, D.C. 20049

This national organization provides a telephone referral service, public-education programs, and financial and legal counseling to bereaved persons. Educational materials also are available.

INDEX

A

Abuse
    alcohol 136
Advocating
    mourner 171-2
Age-level classifications
    children's capacity to understand death 152-3
Aldrich, C.K. 133
Ambivalence
    viewing of the body 124
Anderson, H. 11, 13
Anger
    toward God 45-6
Anniversary
    reactions 113-4
    task for the mourner 113
Anthony, S. 157
Anxiety 42
Aries, P. 150
Assessment
    accomplishing reconciliation needs 141, 144
    common patterns of avoiding grief 141, 143
    complicated grief responses 141, 143
    model for 141-4
    mourner 141-4
    mourner's individual response 141, 142-3
    mourner's physical health 141, 143
Attachment
    influences on Grief 15-23
    making 16
Averill, J.R. 23, 108
Avoidance
    grief 115-20
    heightened 125

B

Barton, D. 92, 108
Bartrop, R. 85

Behavior 15
    grief avoidance 115-20
    grief-related 16
Benefits of funeral
    psychological 147
    social 147
    social group 148
    spiritual 148
Benjamin, B. 85
Bereaved
    See mourner
Bereavement
    definition 1
    research studies 83-5
Bereavement overload 129-30
    caregiver 129
    mourner 129
    nation 129
Body
    viewing the deceased 123-5
Bowlby, J 15, 23, 33, 44, 65, 89, 107, 109, 111

C

Caplan, G. 23
Care, bereavement
    increased interest 7-9
Caregiver
    See helper
    assessable to mourner 166-7
    bereavement 159-63
    bereavement overload 129
    caring 162
    caring for 175-80
    confusion of 177
    congruence 162-3
    contact mourner 166-7
    cynicism of 176
    denial of feelings 178-80
    depression of 176-7
    detachment of 176
    differential diagnosis 137
    disorientation of 177
    empathy 159-61
    encourage recollection of deceased 168

Fitzgerald, R.G. 85
Fluid intake 76
Framework
    loss 11-3
Freud, S. 23, 77, 81, 89, 107
Friedman, S.B. 85
Fulton, R. 108, 131, 133
Funeral
    acknowledgement of feelings of
      loss 149
    changes 148-9
    children attending 154
    distorted 146
    experience 31-2
    expression of feelings and loss
      149
    facilitator 149
    minimized 146
    psychological benefits 147
    purposes 147-50
    ritual 145-50
    social benefits 147
    social group benefits 148
    spiritual benefits 148
    symbolic forms 149
Furman, E. 157

G

Gendin, E.T. 160, 161, 163
Glick, I.O. 46, 65, 127, 128, 133
God's Will
    death 69-70
Going Crazy syndrome 39, 42
Goldberg, I. 133
Gottesman, D.J. 131, 133
Green, M. 85
Grief
    absent 90
    acknowledging the pain 60
    acute 2
    anticipatory 2, 131-3
    assessment 91-5
    assisting as a privilege 181
    avoidance 115-20
    capacity to feel 151
    capacity to understand 151
    catagories of complicated 90-1
    children 151-7
    chronic 91

common dimensions of normal 33-6
complicated 87-108
complicated, response assess-
    ment 143
consequences of avoidance
    119-20
converted 91
crying 127-8
definition 1
differences 25-32
dimension 37, *Figure* 35
displacer 115, 116-7
distinction between normal and
    complicated 87-106
distorted 90-1
duration 109-11
expression 139-40
factors affecting 109
factors influencing 25-32
faith 139-40
features 67-72
framework to assist 96-106
friend to be embraced 140
function of attachment 15-7
funeral ritual 145-50
length of 4-5
minimizer 115, 118
models 33
mood, sudden changes 71
normal *Figure* 55
obsessional review 68
overview of normal experience
    33-65
pathalogical 87-91
patterns of avoidance assessment
    143
postponer 115-6
questioning God's will 69-70
questions for mourners 106-7
replacer 115, 117
response styles 115-20
response to church members
    106-7
rumination 68
search for meaning 68-9
social influences 3-5
somaticizer 115, 118-9
subjective nature 71-2
suicidal thoughts 71
tears 127-8

Meaning
  context of 79-80
  search for 68-9
Medication
  antidepressant 137
  indiscriminent use 136
  mourner 135-8
  use of 135-8
Minimization of feelings
  of caregiver 178-80
Minimizer 115, 118
Mitchell, K.R. 11, 13
Model
  assessment 141-4
  multidimensional 34
  sudden changes 71
Morbidity 83-5
Mortality 83-5
Mourner
  accommodate to the loss 169-70
  advocating 171-2
  alcohol abuse 136-7
  alcohol dependence 136-7
  attitude toward the experience of
    grief 64
  bereavement overload 129
  caring for 162
  complicated grief assessment 143
  contact by caregiver 166-7
  coping with the grief process
    168-9
  crying 127-8
  drug abuse 136-7
  drug dependence 136-7
  educating 171
  empathy with 159-61
  encouraging 172
  guidance 139
  guilt 48-51
  individual response assessment
    142-3
  investing in a new life 170
  listening 170
  medication 135-8
  needs of, *Figure* 35
  needs of reconciliation 110-1
  patterns of avoidance assessment
    143
  physical health assessment 143
  questions regarding grief 106-7

  recollection of deceased 168
  reconciliation needs 74-81
  reconciliation needs accomplish
    ments assessment 144
  referring 172
  resolving secondary losses 168
  respecting 161-2
  silent 5
  supporting 139, 171
  teach you 139-40
  transient thoughts 56
  transitional objects 70-1
  understanding 170
  verbalizing feelings 168
  warmth toward 162
Mourning
  characteristics, *Figure* 35
  definition 1
  tasks of 34, 73-81
Mourning process
  experiencing 88-90
  inaccurate knowledge 88-90
  lack of knowledge 88-90
  reconciling 88-90

N

Nagy, M. 157
Nation
  bereavement overload 129
Needs
  mourner's reconciliation 73-81,
    110-1
Needs of reconciliation 121
Network
  nurturing 76
  social 76
  supportive 76
Numbness 36-9
Nutritional 76

O

Object-relation
  theory 17-8
Objects, transitional 70-1
  definition 70
  mourner 70-1

Wolff, C.T. 85
Worden, J.W. 34, 65, 73, 81, 108, 166, 173

Y

Yearning 39-42
Young, M. 85

Z

Zisook, S. 90, 107

ABOUT

THE

AUTHOR

Alan D. Wolfelt, Ph.D.

Dr. Alan D. Wolfelt, a clinical thanatologist, is the Director of the Center For Loss and Life Transition in Fort Collins, Colorado, and is an Assistant Clinical Professor at the University of Colorado Medical School in the Department of Family Medicine. He lectues and presents workshops throughout the country in the area of thanatology. His practice at the Center For Loss and Life Transition is exclusively in the area of clinical thanatology where he sees many children, adults, and families each year.

Dr. Wolfelt is particularly noted for his work in the grief experience of both the adult and the child. He serves as an educational consultant to hospitals, schools, universities, funeral homes, and a variety of community agencies. He served for several years on the teaching faculty of the Association for Death Education and Counseling and is currently serving on the Professional Advisory Board for the Foundation of Thanatology at Columbia University. Currently, Dr. Wolfelt serves as Editor of the "Children and Grief" section of *Bereavement* Magazine. In 1983, he completed a year long internship in the Department of Psychiatry and Psychology at the Mayo Clinic in Rochester, Minnesota.

Among his publications are the books *Helping Children Cope With Grief* and *Human Relations Training: A Manual For Funeral Home Staffs*. In addition, he is the author of the filmstrips *The Compassionate Friends* and *Children and Death*. Among recent publications is a chapter titled "Death and Grief in the School Setting" in the book *Crisis Intervention for School-Based Helpers*. He has been interviewed by such magazines as *Newsweek, Vogue,* and *Ladies Home Journal.*

WORKSHOP PRESENTATIONS

The Center For Loss and Life Transition specializes in providing quality workshop presentations to a variety of sponsors throughout the country. A wide variety of topics within the area of death, grief, loss, and life transition are available from which to choose. Custom programs are often specifically designed to meet the needs of sponsors. Formats include all day workshops, breakfast and dinner presentations, keynote addresses, and a wide range of other formats.

WHAT PAST PARTICIPANTS HAVE SAID
ABOUT DR. WOLFELT'S WORKSHOPS

"The very *best* seminar I have attended."

"I enjoyed *every* second."

"A very *special* day for me personally and professionally."

"I *learned* more about how to help people with grief in this workshop than I did in my entire seminary training."

To inquire about the Center's Workshops, Training, and Counseling services write or phone:

Center For Loss and Life Transition
Administrative Offices
3735 Broken Bow Road
Fort Collins, CO 80526
Phone (303) 484-1313